AN ELLERY QUEEN JUNIOR MYSTERY

THE PENTHOUSE MYSTERY

By
ELLERY QUEEN

●

Based on the Columbia motion picture
ELLERY QUEEN'S, THE PENTHOUSE MYSTERY

●

GROSSET & DUNLAP
Publishers   NEW YORK

CONTENTS

CHAPTER I

THE NEW OFFICE

WITH HIS thumb Ellery Queen pressed down the lavender button of the buzzer on his desk. For a moment he listened to the resultant rasping noise in the outer office. Removing his thumb, he looked glumly at the pale green enamel buzzer. It was the sort of thing you'd expect to see in a debutante's boudoir, he thought—beside a bed with a taffeta cover.

Mr. Queen shook his head. The buzzer, he decided, was symbolic of female efficiency in general—of Nikki Porter's efficiency in particular. When he wanted his secretary, it was much simpler and more satisfactory to bray out, "Oh, Nikki, come here!"

He had moved into the office suite two weeks before, and even now he couldn't quite understand why he had let Nikki Porter browbeat him into doing it. She must have caught him off guard, somehow.

His gaze wandered resentfully about the im-

I

maculate office: the glossy green metal filing cabinet, the spotless, lacquered linoleum on the floor, the empty scrapbasket by the desk, the painful bareness of the mahogany desk-top. On it was the telephone, a long fountain pen standing at a rakish angle in its swivel holder, an automatic pencil, a pad of paper, two mahogany baskets, one marked OUT, the other IN, in gold lettering, a silver ashtray, and a crystal bowl holding six tearoses.

Ellery Queen absently reached for the buzzer and pressed it again. He longed for the comfortable disorder, the freedom of his own den in the Queen apartment. The den was chaotic, maybe, but it had a personality. It invited you to throw your hat on the floor if you wanted to, or to hang it on the electric fixture. There you could sit on the back of your neck in the Morris chair and hook your heels up on the bookcase. You didn't bother to put things away, you just let everything accumulate on top of the desk, where it was handy when you wanted it.

Efficient! Efficiency, bah! Could you find anything in that metal filing cabinet? You could not. Only Nikki could find anything once it disappeared into its alphabetical complexities. For instance, yesterday he'd wanted that article on Bertillon. Was it under *B?* Certainly not, Nikki had pointed out, with the air of one talking to a child. It was filed under *I,* subdivision *C. Identification—Criminal,* she'd explained.

Now, at home, Ellery Queen had worked out a system that made sense. Everything that was paper went into the double drawer, bottom right, of the desk. It was the depository for newspaper clippings, correspondence, reports, cigar store coupons, old magazines, wrapping paper, and manila envelopes. If you wanted anything, you just burrowed down, and there it was.

What did he want a secretary for, anyway? For years he'd done his own typing. And then a month ago, when he was working on the Braun case, along came Nikki Porter with her big eyes, dark hair, and size-five foot to kick him out of the happy disorder of his den into the frostbitten efficiency of this office. Well, he had no one but himself to blame.

"If you want to submit to female tyranny, that's your business, son," his father, Inspector Queen, of the New York police, had said. "But see that the chit doesn't poke her nose into my affairs. If she wants material for a story, let her look somewhere else. Police business is strictly confidential."

Ellery smiled to himself. Poor Nikki. She really did believe she could write—write mystery stories. Oh well, one thing was sure. She certainly could typewrite—if she ever got around to it.

Ellery looked at the closed door to the outer office and listened.

No sound came from her typewriter. The chapters he'd dictated the day before should have been finished and on his desk—in the IN-basket, rather—when he arrived at the office. But no, they weren't finished—"quite yet."

He leaned forward on the desk, listening. Voices. The muted sound of voices. She was talking to someone. Some girl friend, no doubt. *Chat-chat-chat, gossip, gossip, chat*—on his time. He scowled, put his thumb on the buzzer, and held it down determinedly for thirty seconds. He removed his thumb. The rasping noise stopped simultaneously. He glared at the closed door.

"Oh, Nikki!" he bellowed. "Come here, can't you?"

The door opened slightly. Nikki's brown head popped into sight. Her big, round eyes looked at him innocently, wonderingly.

"Did you call, Ellery?" she asked.

"Yes," Ellery snapped. "Come here."

She stepped into the room and, closing the door, leaned against it. She always looked trim and smart. And she had a figure for clothes. This morning she was wearing a deep blue sharkskin skirt and a rose-colored silk blouse with short sleeves. The rose blouse complemented the soft copper of her suntan.

"Where are chapters six and seven?" Ellery growled.

"Oh, those! I haven't had time. You see—a friend of mine——"

"Yes, I know," he interrupted. "Why can't you see your friends during your noon hour, or in the evening? You're wasting our time, my pet!"

Nikki's eyes grew rounder.

"But you don't understand, Ellery. She's a client."

"Whose client?"

"Why, yours, of course. You're to handle the case."

Ellery Queen groaned. "How many times do I have to tell you I'm a scrivener, not a snoop?"

"Well, you ought to know—if you're not," she said blandly, and then looked hurt. "But I should think that the least you could do is to help my friend when she's in such squiffy trouble."

"Tell her to go to the police," he said, "and get back to your typing. Puh-*leez,* Miss Porter!"

"Ellery, there's a marvelous story in it for you!" said Miss Porter coaxingly.

"I don't need you to get plots for me. Nikki, shoo her out of here, for Pete's sake, and get to work before I've wasted—I mean you've wasted——"

"China," said Nikki mysteriously. "Poor Sheila! She knows about you, Ellery. That's why she came right here."

"China? Sheila? What are you talking about?"

"Mr. Cobb, Sheila's father. He got back from China day before yesterday."

"Well, what of it?"

"He's vanished."

"Vanished?"

"Yes, you know—vanished." Nikki tried out

her most alluring smile—the one that was full of teeth.

"Then tell her to go to the Missing Persons Bureau. What can I do? Be reasonable," moaned Mr. Queen.

"Why can't *you* be reasonable?" said Nikki sternly. "Can't you see people don't just vanish? Not people like Mr. Cobb. Something's happened to him. Sheila knows something awful's happened. You've got to hear her story." Nikki was looking ferocious. "Ellery, you've got——"

She stopped, gasping.

The scream that came from the outer office was so charged with terror that for a moment Ellery Queen sat riveted to the seat. The scream was followed instantly by the sound of a chair striking the floor and a nasty crash—the racket of plate glass cascading and splintering on the terrazzo in the hall.

Ellery Queen bounded across the room. He pushed Nikki aside and flung open the door.

On the floor of the outer office lay the motionless figure of a girl. Her hat, which looked more like a nosegay of forget-me-nots and white violets than a hat, had rolled under the typewriter desk and rested absurdly against the scrapbasket. One arm lay pointing toward the hall door, while her hand clutched her purse with a grip of death.

CHAPTER II

Sheila Cobb

"Sheila!" Nikki was on her knees beside her friend. "Sheila."

Suddenly her jaw dropped.

A red blotch was spreading out on the surface of the girl's gray suède purse. Horrified, Nikki saw the blood creep toward the silver clasp. Then Ellery was kneeling at Sheila's other side. He wiped her face with a towel soaked with cold water. With an end of the wet towel he slapped her face gently.

Sheila's eyes opened. She saw Ellery bending over her and opened her mouth as though she were going to scream again. But then she sighed and sat up.

"What happened, Sheila?" Nikki asked in a tense whisper. "For heaven's sake!"

"Just a minute." Sheila sat holding her head between the palms of her hands. After a moment she said, "I must have fainted."

"But, Sheila, you're hurt. Your wrist is cut."

9

Sheila held out her wrist and looked at it stupidly. Ellery Queen wiped the blood away with the towel. Only a scarlet hairline remained.

"It's just a scratch," he said encouragingly. "Don't worry about it." He helped the girl to her feet. "Nikki, take her into the washroom and fix it up."

"Sheila, come on. I've got a first-aid kit there—bandage, iodine, everything."

"It was silly of me to faint," Sheila murmured.

Ellery went into his office and got the superintendent of the building on the phone. He explained that there had been an accident. The superintendent said there were extra frosted-glass panes and that he would have one put in immediately. As Ellery hung up, Nikki and Sheila came back, Nikki lugging an extra chair. Sheila's wrist was now bandaged, and she had improved on Nature with the co-operation of rouge and lipstick.

"Do you feel up to telling us about it?" Ellery Queen asked gently, putting her into the chair beside his desk.

"Yes, I'm all right now." She looked shaky.

Nikki put her chair close to Sheila's and sat down.

"Someone tried to steal my pocketbook," Sheila began.

"See what he looked like?" Ellery asked.

"No. All I saw was his hand. I was sitting with my back to the door. I'd put my bag on Nikki's desk, right beside me. He came in so quietly that I didn't hear a thing. Then all of a sudden I saw the hand reaching for my pocketbook. I grabbed it—my bag I mean—and the hand grabbed the strap. I hung on with all my might. Then he got his other hand around my neck, from behind. I thought he was going to choke me. That's when I screamed. But I hung onto the bag. I felt the strap break, and that's all I remember. I must have fainted then. Funny, I don't remember getting scratched."

Ellery Queen smiled.

"That's not surprising. And you didn't even get a glimpse of him?"

"No. How could I? He was behind me—strangling me."

Ellery looked out the window for a moment.

Then he turned back and said, quietly, "Miss Cobb, Nikki was starting to tell me about your father, when we were—interrupted."

At the mention of her father, Sheila's own troubles were forgotten.

"Oh, you will help me, Mr. Queen? You will, won't you?" she pleaded.

Her brown curls bobbing on her temples, Nikki nodded vigorously to Ellery.

"Nikki tells me he's disappeared," he said noncommittally. "Tell me about it."

"Well, you see," she began, as though not knowing just where to start, "Father just got back from China. He'd been gone six months."

"What was he doing in China?"

"Oh, he's lived half his life in China. He speaks Chinese—Cantonese and Mandarin. He's always been crazy about the Chinese. You see, he's a ventriloquist."

Ellery blinked.

"A Chinese ventriloquist?" he asked doubtfully.

"No," Sheila laughed. "Dad's an American all right, but he's famous all through the Orient. He does his act in Chinese. It's some sort of satire of the Yuen-Pen drama—that is, Chinese drama. I really don't know what it's all about, but you probably understand. Anyhow, he knows all the important people in China. He has loads and loads of friends. The Chinese adore him. But that's not the point, is it?" She looked at him helplessly.

"Suppose you tell Ellery about his letter," Nikki suggested.

"Oh, yes. You see, I got an air mail letter from him about ten days ago. It said that he would be landing at San Francisco on August tenth and would be in New York four days later, the fourteenth."

"That's today," Ellery said.

"Yes," Sheila nodded. "He asked me to be sure to reserve the penthouse at the Hollingsworth Hotel."

Ellery Queen was surprised. The Hollingsworth was an expensive hotel on Fifth Avenue, in the sixties. Cobb must be a rich man. The penthouse would set him back a pretty penny, he thought. Now, just how could a ventriloquist, in China of all places, make that kind of money?

"Why the Hollingsworth?"

Embarrassed, Sheila hesitated. Then she smiled. It was a proud, candid smile.

"It's been one of Dad's ambitions," she said. "You see, we've always been poor. In a way, the Hollingsworth symbolized success to him, I suppose. When I was a little girl he used to take me riding on the Fifth Avenue buses. Whenever we passed the Hollingsworth, he'd point up at the penthouse and say, 'Sheila, some day you and I are going to live up there—the day my ship comes in.' Well, that's what his letter meant. His ship had come in at last. That was his way of telling me. I knew what he meant—that I was to move out of my apartment in Greenwich Village, and we wouldn't have to worry again, ever."

"But, Miss Cobb," Ellery Queen said, "if your father isn't due until today——"

"But, Ellery," Nikki interrupted. "Mr. Cobb sailed on the *Manchuria*. It was to stop at Yokohama, but it cut out Japan entirely. It got to San Francisco two days early. Mr. Cobb arrived in New York the day before yesterday. Then he vanished."

Ellery turned back to Sheila.

"Are you sure about that?"

"Positive," Sheila said firmly. "When I found out at the hotel that he'd arrived two days ago, I checked up with the steamship company. I suppose he was planning to surprise me. That must have been it. You see we're awfully fond of each other." She looked down at her hands, but Ellery saw the tears. "Ever since mother died—I've tried to take her place. Of course, I can't, but—— The first thing he would have done, if something wasn't terribly wrong, would have been to phone me. And I've called Mr. Walsh, his manager. Father didn't get in touch with him, either. Besides his name is on the hotel register and his clothes are all unpacked. Something must have happened, Mr. Queen. Something must have."

Ellery heard the distress in the girl's voice, he saw it in her eyes, and turned once more to look out the window. Her distress was too real, too personal——

"Ellery, it's black hand," Nikki was saying earnestly. "He was being threatened by a blackmailer."

Ellery swung round.

"What do you mean, Nikki?"

"Sheila," Nikki said, "show him the letters."

Sheila opened her purse. From an inner pocket she took two envelopes and handed them over.

He examined the postmarks: *Grand Central, 11:30 a. m., Aug. 12; Grand Central, 9:45 p. m., Aug. 13.* Both were addressed to Mr. Gordon Cobb, Hollingsworth Hotel, New York City, and the addresses were handprinted with broad black downward strokes, the cross-strokes being narrower.

"Don't you see, Ellery," Nikki asked, leaning over the desk to look at the envelopes, "the addresses have been printed that way so that no one could ever identify the handwriting? Somebody dipped a match or something in ink and wrote with it to disguise the writing. It's black hand." With narrowed eyes, she looked sharply at Ellery.

He turned to the window and held the envelopes up against the light.

"Looks to me as though there wasn't anything in them but a couple of calling cards. Shall we see?" He glanced at Sheila.

"Yes, of course, open them."

Ellery took a paper knife from the desk drawer and slit the tops of the envelopes. From them he extracted two white cards, about three inches by two. He laid them both on the desk before him.

Each bore a legend in the same curious print-ing that had been used to address the envelopes. He read the first inscription aloud: "APPOINTED PLACE, SERPENT."

"There!" said Nikki, triumphantly. "Didn't I tell you? That's the blackmailer's signature, *Ser-pent.*"

Ellery read the second card: "APPOINTED PLACE, PIG." He shook his head and looked at Nikki.

"I don't think even a blackmailer would call himself *Pig,*" he said and grinned. "Do you mind if I keep these awhile?" he asked Sheila.

"Of course not, Mr. Queen."

"Did you plan to move to the Hollingsworth today?"

"Yes, but of course I shan't—now. I went there early this morning to find out if everything was all right and to get my key. I was going to bring my bags uptown this afternoon. But when I found out that Dad had disappeared, I was so up-set I came right here. The morning he arrived, he sent some suits to the cleaner's. No one's seen him since he gave them to the bellboy. You will help me, won't you, Mr. Queen?"

Ellery had jumped from his chair. He was scowling, lost in thought. Suddenly he opened a closet door, took out a gray felt hat and jammed it on his head.

"Well, aren't you coming?" he asked the two girls, as if he were surprised to find them still seated.

Nikki jumped up.

"Coming? But where?"

"To the Hollingsworth!" He started with long strides for the door in the outer office.

Nikki grabbed her hat from the clothes tree and retrieved Sheila's from under the typewriter desk.

"But Ellery, they haven't fixed the window in the door yet."

"That's all right," said Mr. Queen. "If somebody cleaned the whole place out, I'd be very pleased. *Very* pleased!"

CHAPTER III

PENTHOUSE

THE HOLLINGSWORTH was the kind of hotel Mr. Queen invariably associated with white cotton gloves. That was natural enough, he thought to himself as he sat silently between Nikki and Sheila in the taxi, his long legs resting on the folding seat. All its employees wore white cotton gloves—winter, fall, spring, and summer. It was the hotel's trademark.

Even on that hot August afternoon the doorman was wearing a uniform, heavy with gold braid, that would have served very well for an admiral leading a full-dress parade down Fifth Avenue on a blustery January afternoon.

As the taxi drew up to the curb, the doorman unbent to open the door and stepped to one side. Ellery got out and paid the driver. The white-gloved hand shut the cab door and was snapped up to the visor of the doorman's cap in a military salute as Ellery and the two girls started across the sidewalk. A second admiral swung the revolving door. Sheila, not stopping at the office, led the way to the elevators at the rear of the lobby.

"Seventeen," she said to the operator.

The car shot up rapidly. Ellery watched the indicator. *Eight, nine, ten, eleven, twelve, fourteen.* He smiled. No thirteenth floor. And hardly a thirteenth floor in the whole city. Sophisticated New York! The elevator door slid open on well-oiled bearings as the car stopped.

The hall on the seventeenth floor—the roof, as it was called—was only some twenty feet long. Besides the two doors to the elevators, there were only five others. Seventeen A, B, and C were apparently penthouse apartments. At the end of the hall a frosted-glass door, hooked back, led onto the roof. To the right, with a red electric bulb over it, the fifth door was marked "Exit."

Taking the key from her purse, Sheila crossed to 17A and unlocked the door. Nikki and Ellery followed her into the apartment. The door opened directly into the large living room. At the far end were two casement windows on either side of a French door, which opened onto the terrace. The color scheme was rose and gray. A thick rose-taupe carpet of chenille completely covered the floor. The couch and four easy chairs were upholstered in gray velour. The draperies at the windows were of flowered chintz, a rose design predominating. On the desk to the right, a high Colonial secretary, was a vase with pink snapdragons. A telephone stood beside it. As Ellery shut the door, a petal dropped off and fluttered down onto the rose-colored blotting pad.

At the same moment they heard a door close in the room to the left—a bedroom.

Sheila started, for an instant gaping at the open doorway. Then she ran.

"Dad! Oh, Dad! Da——" She stopped stock-still on the threshold.

Ellery and Nikki crossed quickly to her side. Then all three went into the bedroom.

Standing with his back to the closed door was a black-haired man in a white duck uniform with brass buttons, also wearing the inevitable white cotton gloves. He was short and stocky.

"What are you doing here?" Sheila demanded, all color gone from her face.

"Sorry, Miss. I didn't mean to startle you. Mr. Cobb asked me to return his suits as soon as the valet had cleaned them and to hang them up in his closet. You haven't heard from Mr. Cobb yet, Miss?"

"No."

There was something curious in the bellboy's manner. Ellery could not tell what it was about the man that struck him as strange—something indefinable. Despite his uniform and slicked-back dark hair, he just didn't look the type. Perhaps it was the way he slouched. Hollingsworth bellboys stand smartly, like soldiers.

"Sorry, Miss. Excuse me." He went quickly from the room.

A moment later they heard the outer door close.

Ellery went to the closet and opened the door. The closet smelt of cleaning fluid and camphor. From a rod hung an assortment of suits and coats. There were several light gabardines, three worsteds, two heavy tweeds, a dinner jacket, a dress suit, three pairs of white flannels, a winter coat with a fur collar, a lightweight herringbone, and a raincoat.

Ellery put his hand into the pocket of the winter coat. He took out a handful of mothballs and then replaced them.

On the shelf above the rod were a silk-hat box, a brown felt hat, a panama, and a derby, as well as two pairs of white shoes, one of canvas, the other doeskin. On the floor were half a dozen other pairs of shoes, tan, black, and patent leather, and an upended suitcase.

Ellery lifted the suitcase. It was, obviously, empty. He stepped back into the bedroom and turned to Sheila, who was sitting on the bed watching him. She looked worried and tired, but pretty in spite of that. Her blonde hair had a soft warm luster, and her eyes were vivid blue. She must be about Nikki's age, Ellery decided. But how old was Nikki? Eighteen? Nineteen. Twenty-five, maybe. You never could tell about a girl's age. And she had Nikki's trim figure. She looked pathetic and very feminine in her purple print dress with the absurd little nosegay of a hat perched above her forehead, looking as if it were going to fall off any minute.

Ellery smiled sympathetically.

"It looks as if your father had brought his entire wardrobe with him, winter and summer," he said.

She nodded.

"Yes. He was going to stay this time, for good. He wasn't going back to China. And you can see he was planning to stay *here*. He's unpacked everything. The bureau's full of his things."

Ellery went to the bureau, which stood beside a French window. Passing the window, he paused to look out at the terrace. It was about sixteen feet wide, with a brown-tiled floor. The parapet, at least four feet high, was faced with brown tiles, too. He glanced down at the bureau. At one end were Cobb's military hairbrushes, a comb lying between them. At the opposite end, in a green leather frame, was a picture of Sheila. It had been taken some years before. She looked about sixteen. Beside the picture was a purple morocco jewel-box. Its hinged lid stood open, revealing the lavender silk lining. The box was empty.

One after another he opened the bureau drawers and looked into them. Shirts—dozens of them, striped, plain, soft-collared, and dress; white piqué waistcoats, handkerchiefs, socks, underwear. Yes, Mr. Cobb had moved in to stay.

For several moments Ellery stared thoughtfully out the window, along the tops of the apartment houses that extended endlessly up Fifth Avenue. Then suddenly his gaze focused on one of the small square panes. The one just above the door handle had obviously been replaced recently. He stepped closer and touched the putty. The surface was hard. He dug his fingernail into it. Underneath the putty was soft.

"Ellery, what are you doing?" Impatiently Nikki came across to stand beside him.

"Marvelous view," he said, and turned to look about the room.

There were twin beds with a table between them. On the table were a telephone and a reading lamp. The carpet was of the same chenille as the one in the living room. Another table, with an easy chair and a floor lamp beside it, stood at the far end of the room. Between it and the closet stood a large wardrobe trunk, with VENTRO THE GREAT stenciled in red letters across the arched top.

"Why Ventro?" Ellery asked Sheila.

"That's the stage name Dad uses in China."

Ellery crossed to a second door, beside the one

to the closet, and opened it. He glanced about the white-tiled bathroom and then turned back to Sheila.

"How many rooms are there in this apartment?"

"Living room, two bedrooms, two baths, and a kitchenette," she said. "The other bedroom's opposite this—across the living room, I mean. It was to be my room."

"Do you mind if I take a look around?"

"Of course not." Sheila got up quickly.

She and Nikki followed him into the living room. They were halfway across it when the doorbell rang.

Sheila spun round.

"Oh! I wonder——!" she said eagerly, but the vitality of her voice faded almost immediately. "No, Dad would have a key." She hurried toward the door.

A big man in overalls and a cap on the back of his head stood in the doorway with a two-wheeled truck beside him. From his hip pocket he took an order book and flipped the pages.

"Porter," he said. "I came to pick up a trunk to be sent out express, Miss. Where is it?"

"There's a trunk in the other room," Sheila began, "but——"

"Where's the trunk to be expressed to?" Ellery asked.

The porter looked in his book.

"Mr. Gordon Cobb, Blackstone Hotel, Chicago. Collect."

Sheila led the way into the bedroom. Ellery, Nikki, and the porter, wheeling the truck, followed.

The porter grasped the leather handle on top of the trunk and pulled. The trunk barely moved. He pulled again, harder. The trunk was slowly ended over onto the truck.

Odd that it should be so heavy, Ellery thought. The amount of clothing Cobb had unpacked should have about emptied it. The only other pieces of baggage besides the trunk were the silk-hat box and the suitcase. He came to a sudden decision.

"Hold it," Ellery Queen said. "I'm not shipping the trunk after all. I've changed my mind."

Sheila stared at him in astonishment. The porter took off his cap and scratched his head. He shrugged.

"Well, you're the boss, Mister." Mumbling, he started for the door.

They heard the truck bang across the doorsill, and the door to the hall close.

Nikki looked with amazement at Ellery.

"But, Ellery, why did——"

Ellery interrupted her.

"Miss Cobb, would you mind going down to the office and asking if your father left orders for expressing his trunk?"

"Oh!" Sheila gave a little gasp. "Of course. But I'll phone."

Ellery caught her arm as she started for the phone.

"Wait," he said. "I'd rather that you went down and saw the head porter personally. Ask him when your father gave the order. Find out all about it."

"Of course," she agreed. "I hadn't thought of ——Oh, of course." She hurried out of the room.

As soon as he heard the outside door close, Ellery darted into the closet. In a moment he was back with a metal shoetree and a heavy hobnail shoe.

"What in the world are you going to do?" Nikki demanded, wide-eyed.

"Snap the lock." He slipped the lip of the shoe-tree under the lock of the trunk.

Gripping the toe of the shoe, he struck the lock with the heel. At the third blow there was a sharp metallic snap, and the lock flew open. He unfastened the catches and started to open the trunk. It was a standing wardrobe trunk that parted in the middle, one half composed of drawers and compartments swinging out like a door, while the other half, provided with hangers for suits and coats, remained stationary. As Ellery released the catches, the movable half swung out of its own accord, impelled by the pressure of something inside.

A man's body slumped out of the trunk. It rolled half over, onto its back. The gray, distorted face with sightless eyes stared up at them. The fingers of a clenched fist slowly uncurled. Then the whole body seemed to sag and lie limp, while the lower jaw dropped open.

Quickly Ellery turned to Nikki. With dilated eyes she was staring down at the corpse. Her face was as gray as the dead man's. She was clutching her throat with both hands, and trying desperately to say something. Her lips moved, but no sound came from them.

Ellery grabbed her arm and pulled her into the living room. He shut the door and ran to the phone on the desk.

"Operator—Operator, police headquarters. Step on it, Operator!"

CHAPTER IV

INSPECTOR QUEEN

To NIKKI fell the unpleasant task of telling Sheila that her father was dead and, what was more horrible, had been murdered. As soon as she knew, Sheila had pleaded with Ellery to be allowed to see her father, but he refused definitely, and locked the door. Then Nikki had taken her, sobbing and hysterical, into the empty bedroom.

A half hour after Ellery's call to police headquarters, his father, Inspector Richard Queen, and Sergeant Velie arrived at the penthouse. Inspector Queen was a wiry little man with a straggling gray mustache and quick, birdlike motions. Ellery made two of him.

Sergeant Velie's worship of the inspector was well known at Centre Street. "Your dad's a little old coot," he was fond of telling Ellery, "but a damn tough little old coot. He can take it and, oh boy, he can dish it out." No more perfect counterfoil for the frail, dynamic little inspector could be imagined; for Sergeant Velie was a colossus. He stood six feet four, and possessed all the physical charm of a gorilla.

By the time they arrived, Sheila had recovered sufficiently from the shock to tell the inspector the little she knew about the events preceding her father's death. Then she had retired once more with Nikki to the bedroom.

The inspector and Ellery returned to Cobb's room to continue the examination while Velie telephoned the Medical Examiner's office, the fingerprint men and photographers, and Walsh, Cobb's publicity manager. With Walsh he was tough.

"Well, son," the inspector said, looking down at the body on the floor by the trunk, "what do you make of it? It looks to me as if he'd been strangled."

"Yes," Ellery agreed. "My guess is either that someone broke in from the terrace and waited here to kill Cobb, or that Cobb walked in on the murderer unexpectedly." He steered his father across to the French window and pointed out the recently replaced pane by the door handle. "Judging by the condition of the putty," he said,

"I'd say that pane was put in a couple of days ago, and there's a funny thing about it. There's not a fingerprint on the putty or the glass. Whoever heard of a glazier who didn't leave his marks all over the place?"

"The maid may have cleaned the glass after it was put in," the inspector observed dryly.

"Right," said Ellery, "but if I know anything about the management here, the putty would have been painted to match the trim long before this."

The inspector pursed his lips.

"I'll ask the manager about that." He picked up the morocco jewelry box from the bureau. "Well, either the motive was robbery or the murderer wants us to think it was. If it was, this box must have contained something mighty valuable. There's over a thousand dollars in Cobb's wallet, and a thief doesn't pass up money like that unless the rest of the haul's plenty, believe me."

"I gather from what Sheila Cobb says that her father must have made a small fortune just before he left China. She's been living in a little place down in the Village. And now Cobb suddenly blossoms out at the Hollingsworth. You'd think

——" Ellery stopped as the door to the living room opened.

"The bellboy's here, Chief," Velie announced.

"Bring him in," the inspector grunted.

The bellboy turned nearly as white as his uniform as he came into the room and saw the body on the floor.

"What's your name?" the inspector snarled.

Without taking his gaze from the body, the man answered, "Jim Sanders, sir."

"Look at me!"

Sanders jerked again and faced Inspector Queen.

"How long you been working here?"

Sanders swallowed.

"Two days, sir."

"Recognize the body?"

"Yes, sir. It's Mr. Cobb." He glanced at the body and then quickly looked away.

"When did you last see him?"

"When he gave me two suits for the valet."

"When was that?"

"The day before yesterday, sir. Friday. About noon. I'd only just started in. The call came and the captain sent me up."

o

"What was Cobb doing?"

"Unpacking, sir. Hanging up his clothes in the closet. He told me when the suits were cleaned to put them in the closet."

"Did you see him after that?"

"No, sir."

"What's the manager's name, Sanders?"

"Mr. Parkman, sir."

"All right, tell Parkman I want to see him. And keep your lip buttoned about Mr. Cobb's death."

"Yes, sir." Sanders practically ran.

Ellery and the inspector followed him into the living room. As Sanders went out, Dr. Sam Prouty, the Assistant Medical Examiner, arrived with the police photographer and the fingerprint expert.

Dr. Prouty, an old friend of the inspector, had a personal grudge against murder victims, as though they got themselves murdered purposely in order to make work for him. A cadaverous sort of person himself, and sarcastic, he perpetually complained about being overworked.

"Well," he demanded petulantly, pushing his hat onto the back of his head and taking a cold, badly chewed cigar butt, two inches long, from between his teeth, "what now? Another stiff, I suppose."

The inspector jerked his thumb toward the bedroom.

"In there. Stop grousing and get to work." He turned to the other two men and gave them orders.

Ellery went along with Prouty. In a few minutes the inspector joined them in the bedroom.

"Well," he asked, looking at Prouty when the doctor had finished his preliminary examination, "what's the verdict?"

"Strangulation," Prouty said, getting up from his knees and whisking them with his felt hat. "The hombre was strangled by someone with long fingers and sharp fingernails. As though strangling him wasn't enough, the killer scratched the back of his neck."

Prouty had rolled the body over. Ellery got down and examined the scratch. It was a mere hairline with a few drops of coagulated blood. With a shock he realized that it was precisely the same kind of mark that had been left on Sheila's wrist!

"How long's he been dead?" Inspector Queen asked.

"Two days at least. Well, *c'est la guerre.*" Prouty picked up his cigar butt from the edge of the bureau, stuck it into the corner of his mouth, and started for the door.

"Hey, hold on there, Voltaire," the inspector called after him. "How soon can you do a post mortem?"

Prouty turned, scowling.

"When I can get to it! Every man bears his cross—mine has the initials R. Q. on it. Well, send him down to the morgue. He's got to get on line." He chuckled suddenly and strolled out of the room. The inspector shook his head.

Velie came into the room, grinning.

"His Nibs, the manager, is at hand," he announced.

"I'll see him in the living room," Inspector Queen said.

Following his father, Ellery Queen closed the door to the bedroom.

Parkman, judging from his manner and costume, considered himself as important as a high-ranking officer in the diplomatic service—an ambassador or a minister, at least. As they came into the room, he was taking a white silk handkerchief from the tail pocket of his morning coat. He patted his cheek with it and then stood with his thumb in the pocket of his light gray waistcoat. In his tie, a shade or two darker than the waistcoat, nestled a large pearl stickpin. His hair shone like his patent leather shoes.

"Inspector Queen," he said stiffly, "I understand that you wish to see me. I am shocked, deeply shocked, at this unfortunate occurrence, I assure you. The reputation of the Hotel Hollingsworth is——"

"Skip it," the inspector said. "I don't want this to get into the papers any more than you do. So tell your help to keep their mouths shut. What I wanted to ask you was about your bellboy, James Sanders. He says he's been working here only two days. What do you know about him?"

"Why!" Parkman exclaimed, apparently taken aback. "He had the best of references. Naturally the Hollingsworth——"

"The best of what references?" the inspector interrupted.

"Why—from the chief steward of the Amer-
ica-and-Orient Line, Oscar Bergen. He's the chief
steward on the *Manchuria*. He was headwaiter
here for years, and Oscar wouldn't have given
Sanders a letter to me if he weren't completely
trustworthy and efficient."

At the mention of the ship on which Gordon
Cobb had crossed the Pacific, the inspector and
Ellery exchanged glances. The inspector immediately changed the subject and asked if a new
pane had been put in a French window in the
suite recently. Parkman was assuring the inspector that nothing of the sort had been reported to him, as it inevitably would have been, et
cetera, when Ellery, looking bored, strolled out
of the room.

A few minutes later he was at the office in the
lobby examining the hotel register. He made a
list of the twenty-odd arrivals since August
twelfth, and then went to the head porter's desk.
The head porter smilingly accepted the bill that
Ellery handed him with the list. He read the list
carefully.

Yes, he had noticed the steamship stickers on

Mr. Cobb's luggage. That same day two others had arrived, who also had crossed on the *Manchuria,* Count Brett and a Miss Olga Otero. He checked both names on the list and handed it back to Ellery. The count's apartment was in the penthouse 17B. Miss Otero had taken room 766.

By the time Ellery got back to the Cobb apartment, Parkman had gone. The inspector stopped pacing the floor as Ellery entered the room.

"El," he said, wrinkling his forehead and plucking at his mustache, "it's a mighty queer coincidence about Sanders having been on the *Manchuria* with Cobb."

"That's not the half of it, Dad." Ellery Queen handed the list to his father. "The two that are checked were on the same crossing. The count's parked in 17B. That's right next door. And that's not all. Take a look at these." From the envelopes he took the two cards that had been mailed to Mr. Cobb.

"APPOINTED PLACE, SERPENT," the inspector read aloud. "APPOINTED PLACE, PIG. What in time?"

"I think you'd better look for a Chinese."

"Chinaman?"

"A Chinese. There has to be a Chinese in it, Dad."

"Now, hold on, son. Not so fast with your tricks—"

"You've got to find the Chinese," Ellery continued, "and the thing that's missing."

"What's missing?"

"Something of Gordon Cobb's. It's your most important clue."

"Missing? Missing?" The inspector's eyebrows lowered. "You mean the jewelry?"

"No. You're not getting feeble-minded, are you, Dad? What's so conspicuously missing that only a blind man would skip it?"

"Ellery, sometimes you get in my hair! *What's* missing?"

"Sorry, Dad. I didn't mean to annoy you. Don't you see that——"

The door to Sheila's bedroom was suddenly flung open. Wide-eyed, she stood on the threshold.

"Mr. Queen, quick," she cried. "Quick, quick."

Ellery sprang toward her.

"What is it?" he demanded.

She pointed hysterically to the open French window in the bedroom.

"Nikki," she gasped. "And a man's out there!"

Ellery sprinted out onto the terrace.

CHAPTER V

NIKKI WAS not in sight. To the left, about twenty feet beyond the door to Cobb's room, the terrace came to an end. To the right there was a row of tubs placed close together and planted with boxwood, so as to form a hedge nearly shoulder-high. Beyond the boxwood were tall palms. Ellery punched an opening in the hedge and peered through. The terrace continued to the east for a hundred feet. Still no sign of Nikki.

He squeezed through the boxwood and ran to the end of the terrace. There, in a right angle, it turned south. As he ran round the corner he saw her. Animatedly but safely, she was talking with a short, baldheaded man in a Palm Beach suit. Ellery walked toward them.

As Ellery approached, the man raised a monocle to his eye and stared.

"I shall report this to the management, and I hope you will do as well, Mademoiselle," he was saying heatedly.

43

Seeing the stranger stare past her, Nikki turned.

"Oh, Ellery," she said breathlessly.

"What's wrong, Nikki?" Ellery asked.

"A Peeping Tom was snooping outside Sheila's room——"

"Pardon," the stranger interrupted. "I see you have also been disturbed." He bowed slightly to Ellery. "We foreigners are not accustomed to the insolence of gangsters. The fellow nearly knocked me down. Pardon, I introduce myself. Count Claude Alexandre Brett." He made a quick, stiff little bow from the waist.

Ellery could not place the man's foreign accent. It was not French, German, or Italian. Rather, he decided, it was the accent of a person who had from childhood spoken several languages fluently, so that the characteristics of no one predominated. He took an instant dislike to M. le Comte.

"What did he look like?" Ellery asked.

"I didn't see him," Nikki said quickly. "Sheila saw a hand come through the hedge outside her room. His face was hidden. It scared her half to death. All she could do was gasp and point. And

I saw the hedge go together again. I ran out onto the terrace and chased around here."

"Pardon," the count said impatiently. "I saw
the fellow—that is, I saw his back. I had but stepped out of my apartment for the fresh air. I was
admiring the view yonder." He waved his arm
to the east and south in a gesture that swept the
horizon from the East River to the Chrysler
Building. "Suddenly he bumps against my
shoulder and does not stop to apologize. He leaps
the railing like a rabbit. I do not know that there
is the roof beyond the railing and I think he commit suicide. But no, there is a door yonder that
goes into the hall where are the elevators." He
brushed some imaginary specks off his shoulder
and sleeve.

"What did he look like?" Ellery repeated.

"He was short and stocky." The count spoke
slowly but positively. "He was wearing a brown
suit. That is all I see. No—he has a black mustache."

"Well, come along, Nikki," Ellery took her
elbow. "He must be out of the building by now.
There's nothing we can do about it."

"I trust that you, too, will lodge a complaint with the manager. I go to do so at once," Brett said.

As they turned to go, Inspector Queen came hurrying round the corner. He looked Brett over, from the points of his waxed, black mustache to the sharp toes of his black shoes, and then turned inquiringly to Ellery.

Ellery introduced the count to his father and then told him tersely what had happened.

The inspector grunted and turned back to Brett. The count's monocle raised his right eyebrow in a way that made him look both supercilious and impatient. Looped about his neck, a black ribbon dangled from his eyeglass.

"You reached San Francisco recently on the *Manchuria,* did you not, Mr. Brett?"

The count became even more stiff.

"That is so."

"Did you happen to meet a fellow-passenger named Cobb?"

"Cobb?—Cobb?" Brett frowned thoughtfully down at the brown tiles. "Ah, I remember. There was a man named Cobb. Some sort of professional entertainer, I was told. No, I did not meet him.

Most certainly, I did not." The count's manner implied that he would associate with no one of so inferior a social standing. "Why do you inquire, may I ask?"

"He's been murdered, that's why," the inspector murmured.

The count gaped at Inspector Queen. His lips described an O the size of his monocle. Then the eyeglass fell and swung like a pendulum at the end of the black ribbon.

It was a moment or two before he could speak. "Murdered? Ach! *Murdered?*"

If Cobb and Brett had been complete strangers, Ellery thought, the count's violent reaction to the inspector's announcement was hard to explain.

But Brett quickly recovered his poise.

"Oh, monsieur," he said suavely, "then you are a police inspector, is it so?"

"Did you think I was a customs' inspector? How long are you planning to stay at the Hollingsworth?"

"Possibly a week, possibly longer."

"Good," said the inspector. "I'll have a talk with you later." He nodded abruptly and started back toward the Cobb suite.

"I don't like the looks of that bird, Ellery," his father said as they walked along the terrace.

"What was he doing when you ran into him on the terrace, Nikki?" Ellery asked. "Try to remember exactly."

"Picking up a cigarette," Nikki said promptly. "He tossed it over the parapet as I came up to him. He said the man knocked it out of his mouth when they collided."

"Either he was the snooper himself or he's protecting a confederate," Ellery said.

"How do you figure that out?" Nikki asked, annoyed.

"Because he said he saw only the man's back —and then told us that the man had a black mustache. It's not likely the snooper has grown a mustache on the back of his head."

"Oh," said Nikki, deflated.

"He mentioned a black mustache because he has one himself."

"I don't follow you, son," the inspector said.

"He couldn't be sure that someone hadn't got a glimpse of the person who was peeping through the boxwood. If someone saw a face with a black mustache and Brett said that the man he saw was clean-shaven, then his whole story would collapse."

Sergeant Velie was towering over the palms by the boxwood hedge as they approached it.

"Chief," he said, "Walsh is here. Miss Cobb's with him in the parlor."

Harry Walsh got up from a chair when Inspector Queen and Ellery went into the living room, Velie having remained on guard by the French window in Sheila's room. He was a squat, middle-aged man with sparse gray hair, spectacles, and well-rounded stomach. To judge from his shortness of breath, his ruddy, blotched complexion, and his tendency to sweat, he was a faithful disciple of Bacchus. He mopped his face as he stood up, then extended his hand to the inspector and to Ellery. The hand was flabby and damp.

"This is the most dreadful thing, Inspector. Worse than dreadful."

Walsh resumed his seat. Ellery sat down and stretched his long legs. Nikki was on the arm of Sheila's chair. Perched on the edge of an armchair, Inspector Queen looked appraisingly at Walsh.

"Do you know if Cobb had any enemies?"

"Enemies! Absolutely not!" Walsh said emphatically. "Cobb was one of the most likable fellows I ever knew. Popular with everyone. Full of stories. Made folks laugh. Everybody liked him; loved him, in fact!"

"Did Cobb write you that he was returning to this country on the *Manchuria?*"

"No, he didn't; and that's a queer thing," Walsh said, frowning.

"Mr. Walsh was really more in his confidence than I was," Sheila said. "It's awfully strange about Dad's not letting him know."

Walsh turned to Sheila.

"Well, Sheila," he said diplomatically, "after all, I was his publicity manager. Naturally he would keep me informed only about matters of business."

"When did you last hear from him?" the inspector asked.

"About six weeks ago."

"What did Cobb say then? What did he write about?"

"Just a note—a memorandum about his earnings."

"Did he ever speak of a Count Brett to you?"

"Brett?" Walsh mopped behind his ears. "Brett? Nope. No, he never did."

"In his letter, did he mention any jewelry?"

Walsh raised his eyebrows.

"Why, as a matter of fact, he did—confidentially. But there's no reason for its being confidential now." He stuffed the wet handkerchief into his pocket, got out a fresh one, and wiped his spectacles. He turned once more toward Sheila. "My dear," he said sympathetically, "your father wrote that he had found a very old and very precious jade necklace for you. He wanted to surprise you and asked me not to mention it. But now, of course—I'm so sorry, Sheila. So dreadfully sorry."

Sheila was having a hard time being a heroine. Suddenly she gulped and buried her face in her hands.

The inspector looked uncomfortable.

"I should have known better," he muttered self-reproachfully. "Nikki, take Miss Cobb into the other room, please."

Nikki took Sheila, still sobbing, into the bedroom.

After ten minutes' further questioning, Walsh left, promising to keep in touch with Inspector Queen.

"Well, son," the inspector said to Ellery as the door closed behind Walsh, "I didn't get much out of him. But one thing's important. That's the jade necklace. It supplies the motive. Theft. Find the necklace and we find the murderer."

"No soap, Dad."

"Huh?" The inspector arched his gray eyebrows.

"I'll admit the necklace was probably in the jewel box. I'll admit it's been stolen. But it wasn't what the thief or thieves were after. They took it incidentally. Why, I don't know, because they didn't bother about the thousand in currency. The necklace doesn't tie in with the rest of the picture. The thieves were after something a lot more important than the necklace, though they seem to have taken a fancy to it. But why is another of Cobb's possessions missing—one that no ordinary thief would lift? And it doesn't explain the Chinese correspondent."

"Chinese correspondent?"

"Yes, the cards. The Serpent-Pig gentleman."

"Now, El. You and your Chinese." The inspector chuckled. *"Cherchez le chinois,"* he said with an appalling French accent. "All right, you search for the Chinese. Personally, I'm going to *cherchez* the *femme."*

"Miss Otero?"

"Your astuteness sometimes surprises me, Ellery. But most of the time you talk like the stuffed owl called Ellery Queen in your so-called mystery stories."

The phone rang. The inspector went to it and took up the receiver.

"All right, Mr. Parkman, thank you," he said after a moment, and hung up. "I sent for this Otero woman. She's on her way up."

Almost as he spoke, the doorbell rang.

CHAPTER VI

MISS OTERO

FRAMED in the doorway, Miss Olga Otero would
have been a fit subject for a portrait by Sargent,
Ellery Queen decided. Her long, dark eyelashes
—heavy with mascara—and her blue-black hair,
brushed back off her high forehead and temples
and held close to her head, made her white skin
look whiter than white. She was dressed completely in black, and seemed to have been molded
into the black silk dress. Black net gloves reveal-
ed the whiteness of her fingers. Jet earrings
flashed darkly.

Black and white, Ellery thought. A study in
black and white, and with just one startling, em-
phatic dash of scarlet—her mouth. The eyebrows,
two fine, arched lines, were mere pencil strokes.
She raised them slightly.

"Inspector Queen?" Her voice was deep,
throaty, but pleasant and soft. The scarlet lips
parted, showing beautifully symmetrical teeth.

Her accent wasn't Russian, but close to Russian. She gave too much value to the *o* in "inspector," and rolled the *r* a little.

Inspector Queen blinked several times, as if to clear his vision and assure himself that the woman wasn't an apparition.

"Come in, please, Miss Otero," he said.

"*O-tai-ro*," she corrected him, stressing each syllable equally. "You wish to talk with me, I am informed by Mr. Parkman."

"Yes, yes. Sit down, please." He motioned toward a chair.

As she passed Ellery, he inhaled a strong heady perfume.

Her poise would be hard to shake, Ellery decided, and wondered if she was thirty, thirty-five, or forty. No one would ever know her age, that was certain. And it didn't matter. In sophistication she was older than the Sphinx—but, he hoped, lacked the Sphinx's wisdom. She was a thoroughly dangerous woman. She knew it and wanted you to know it. That was her fascination. He offered her a cigarette. She looked at him and shook her head, but smiled. She opened her patent-leather purse. From a jet box she took a long, gold-tipped cigarette. Ellery held a match.

She smiled again, glancing up through her long lashes.

"Well, Inspector Queen?" she inquired, turning to him.

"I understand that you were acquainted with Mr. Gordon Cobb," the inspector said.

"We returned from the Orient on the same ship, Inspector. I made his acquaintance on the *Manchuria.*"

"Are you an American citizen, Miss Otero?"

She shook her head, took a puff of her cigarette, and inhaled deeply. Again Ellery smelt the perfume—musk, he decided. Even the tobacco must be scented with it.

"I have a League of Nations passport. I am a refugee. I have no country." She sighed and lowered her darkened eyelids.

"Did you know Mr. Cobb well?"

"We talked together much. We were seated at the same table in the dining salon, and our steamer chairs happened to be together. Yes, we talked together very much. On a sea voyage one easily becomes acquainted."

"Did he mention any special mission he had undertaken?"

"Mission? What does that mean, mission?"

"—some special or unusual reason for making the trip to the States?"

"But no! He was happy to be returning to his country, that is all. He was gay. He said nothing about a special *meeshun,* as you say."

"Did you meet a Count Brett while you were on the boat?"

"Count Claude Alexandre Brett." She smiled. "Yes, I met the count. I believe he is stopping at this hotel."

"How did you happen to choose this hotel?"

"This is my first visit to New York. I did not know the hotels. Mr. Cobb recommended the Hollingsworth. So I came here."

"Did he recommend it to the count, too?"

Again she smiled.

"I think that is most unlikely. Mr. Cobb did not like Count Brett. He said the count was what he calls—'fathead.' I think he means snob. I think the count did not like Mr. Cobb, either. They did not speak together."

Ellery took a package of cigarettes from his pocket. There were about four left, he saw, but he crumpled them and the package into a wad.

He got up and, crossing to the desk, threw the wad into the scrapbasket.

"Excuse me," he said, nodding to the others, and without further explanation went into the hall and closed the door.

He rang the elevator bell impatiently.

"Ninth floor," he said, getting into the car a few minutes later.

On the ninth floor he went quickly to the fire-stair and ran down two flights. On the seventh floor, opposite the elevators, a plaque indicated that rooms 701-731 were to the west and 732-770 to the east. He hurried along the corridor in the direction of the higher numbers.

Now if he only got a break, he was thinking. It was a pretty slim chance, but worth taking. If he didn't get a break, then his father could get a warrant and do it legally. But that would take time—the hotel manager didn't look particularly co-operative.

Oh, well, sometimes he was lucky.

The maid was cleaning in room 750. The door was ajar. Her pass key, with a long metal tag hanging from it, was in the lock. Noiselessly he took it out and ran on down the hall, which

turned to the right. He stopped before 766. For
a moment he listened, and then quickly unlocked
the door and went in. The room was redolent
with the strong pervasive scent of musk.

It wouldn't be an easy thing to hide, he told
himself. It would about fill a suitcase . . . the
missing object.

One after another he opened the bureau drawers. Clothes. Nothing but clothes. He searched
the closet. More clothes. Before the window stood
a trunk. A red and white tag hung from the
strap handle: s. s. MANCHURIA. CABIN. He pulled
up the lid. The top tray was empty. Reaching
down, he opened the box, blinked, and then
grinned.

Keys. Yale keys. Corbin keys. Keys, keys, keys.
All apparently classified. Three files. A pair of
pliers. A miniature vise. So Miss Olga Otero fan-
cied herself as a locksmith. Well, that was something to know.

A few minutes later Ellery Queen was back at
the penthouse apartment. As he came in, he was
breaking open a new package of cigarettes.

"Had to skip down to the cigar stand," he explained.

"Well, that's all, Miss Otero," his father was saying. "Thank you for coming up."

Miss Otero got up. She turned to Ellery.

"Inspector Queen has told me. It is sad, very sad. Mr. Cobb was so full of vitality. So much *joie de vivre!* It is very sad." She lowered her dark eyelashes as she passed Ellery, who had opened the door for her.

After he had closed it, the air was still heavy with musk.

"If you don't mind, Dad," he said, "I'll open the French windows and let in some fresh air."

Following his father out onto the terrace, Ellery told him about searching Miss Otero's room and finding the locksmith's kit.

The inspector wrinkled his forehead and impatiently whisked his straggly mustache away from his lips.

"There's a lawful way to do things, son, and an unlawful way. I don't like the way you barge into places. Some day you're going to get yourself into trouble."

"All right, Dad. There weren't any witnesses, so there's no use your bringing charges of trespassing against me. You couldn't prove a thing.

Anyhow, I've got to get back to the office." He looked at his watch. "Two o'clock. I've wasted half the day."

"Look here, El. You're not walking out on me?" the inspector asked anxiously.

"Now look, Dad," said Mr. Queen firmly. "I was feeble-minded enough to let Nikki and this Cobb girl——"

"El, can't you see I'm worried? We're not getting anywhere. Here we have four possible suspects. Sanders, the bellboy, may have followed Cobb here from China. It's possible that Count Brett did, too. I think you're right about his being the snooper a while ago. He had the opportunity to kill Cobb. He could have walked around by the terrace and broken the pane while Cobb was out, and then waited for him—or have been caught stealing the necklace when Cobb returned unexpectedly. Then there's Cobb's manager, Walsh. He's holding something back. We can be pretty sure Walsh knew Cobb was arriving on the twelfth. According to Miss Cobb, he's always been in her father's confidence. And now you come with your talk about Miss Otero. She's a slick article, all right."

"And the Celestial," Ellery said. "Don't forget the Celestial."

"Now, El," his father said irritably, "why do you keep on talking about a Chinaman? There isn't any Chinaman."

"Well, Dad," drawled Ellery, "if I were handling this case, I'd wire San Francisco and find out if there was a Chinese aboard the *Manchuria*. And I'd have the deck steward and the dining-room steward interviewed to find out if Miss Otero tipped them respectively to have herself seated at Cobb's table and his steamer chair put beside hers—though maybe, so far as that's concerned, she just switched the name-cards herself. But I'm off. I've got to see if I can't somehow induce Nikki to do a little work. It takes about a week to get a day's work out of that girl." He strode off toward Sheila's room.

Velie grinned as Ellery Queen came through the French window.

"Still on the scent, Bloodhound?"

Ellery ignored him.

"Come along, Nikki."

"Come along where?" Nikki sat up straight.

"To the office. Where do you suppose? To Jones Beach?"

"Oh, but I've laid off for the day. I'm going home with Sheila. You don't think I'd leave her alone, do you? Besides we haven't had any lunch."

"Please, Mr. Queen, let Nikki come with me."

"Of course he will. It's all settled."

Ellery sighed.

"All right, all right. But do you mind dropping me off at the office on the way downtown?"

As the cab pulled away from the curb in front of the hotel, Ellery Queen said, "Let me have your vanity case, Nikki."

Unquestioning, she handed him her compact.

"Just a touch of powder on the nose would help, Ellery. Not too much, or it will show."

The cab turned east on Sixty-sixth Street.

Holding the mirror of the compact before his face, Ellery was looking into it.

"It's his vanity," Nikki said to Sheila. "He loves to look at himself."

Ellery was too intent to hear.

"Yep, I knew it!" he said after a moment.

"When we came out, Brett was watching from the drugstore. He got into the cab behind us. He's following." He leaned forward to speak to the driver. "Listen, driver, when you get to Madison, turn right. The light's red, but it doesn't matter. I'll pay the fine if you're caught. Then full speed for a block south. Turn west on Sixty-fifth and slow up while I jump out. Then keep going. Don't stop."

CHAPTER VII

A FRIENDLY GAME

THE MOMENT the cab had rounded the corner of Sixty-fifth Street, Ellery Queen leaped out. The taxi departed with a burst of speed, but was stopped at Fifth Avenue, waiting for the lights to change, when Brett's cab turned the corner from Madison Avenue.

Seated in a third taxi, parked by the curb, Ellery watched the driver of the following cab slow up as he evidently saw the car ahead waiting at the intersection.

The lights changed from red to green. The traffic started west.

"All right, step on it," Ellery said to his driver. "Don't let him out of your sight."

As they started down Fifth Avenue, Ellery Queen realized that there was little chance of Brett's discovering that he was being followed. He would be too intent upon watching the car in which were the two girls—and, supposedly, Ellery Queen.

They continued down the Avenue to Eighth
Street, where the procession turned west. On
Sixth Avenue they headed south again as far as
Fourth Street, and again made a right turn.

"Now, take it easy," Ellery said, leaning forward. "The first car's likely to stop somewhere
along here."

His prophecy proved correct. In the middle of
the third block it stopped before a red brick house.
Nikki and Sheila got out. Sheila had apparently
passed a bill through the window. On the sidewalk she held out her hand to the driver for her
change. Brett's cab passed the girls' taxi at a
snail's pace.

Ellery wondered what the count's sensations
were when he discovered that his quarry had
vanished—or was his purpose to find out where
Sheila lived? Apparently it took him several
moments to decide what to do. The cab loafed all
the way to Eighth Avenue. Then it started north
with sudden energy, Ellery's cab close behind. It
continued on Eighth Avenue until it reached the
Fifties, and finally turned west.

"Looks like the guy ahead's fixing to stop,"

Ellery's driver said out of the corner of his mouth.

The cab ahead had slowed down and was running close to the curb.

Ellery passed a five-dollar bill through the front window.

"All right. Remember what I told you."

"O. K., boss." The driver put up the flag.

Ellery slipped down on the floor, out of sight, as the car ahead stopped in front of a shabby brownstone apartment house. He felt his own cab slowly come to a stop beside Brett's.

"Hey, Bud," Ellery heard his man say to the other driver, "know where the nearest gas station is? I ain't got more'n a cupful."

"Couple of blocks up Ninth Avenue. Northwest corner."

"Thanks. How they comin'?"

"Lousy."

"Well, cheer up, Buddy, it looks like rain."

The cab jerked forward, turned the corner onto Ninth Avenue, and stopped.

Ellery got up quickly, and stepped out of the cab.

"Your guy rang the second bell from the bottom, on the last row—the inside row, that is," the driver told him.

"Thanks." Ellery started back for the brownstone building.

In the vestibule there were four vertical rows of bells. On the card opposite the second button of the last row *R. M. Smith* had been scribbled in pencil. Ellery peered through a glass door into a dingy hall lit by a feeble unshaded electric bulb. There were four apartments to the floor. Smith's would be on the second floor rear, he decided. It was an old building, built some time in the 'nineties. That was all to the good. There wouldn't be any inside fire-stairs; only an outside fire escape at the rear.

Ellery went through the narrow passage between the apartment house and the adjacent warehouse. It was partly blocked by empty ashcans. In the court behind the building he looked up at the second-story windows. An iron fire escape, the lower section of which hung about twelve feet above the ground because of a heavy balance at the upper end, went up the middle of the wall. At each floor a grilled landing extended to right and left past the windows. The landings on the upper floor were draped with bedding, put out to air in the sun, but the one at the second floor was bare. The shades at the windows to the right, which particularly interested Ellery, were drawn about four-fifths of the way down—to the level of the rows of empty flower pots standing on the windowsills.

He went back to the passageway and returned with one of the empty ashcans. Standing on it, he could just reach the bottom rung of the balanced ladder. He pulled it down slowly and started up. Lying flat on the platform, he worked his way toward the flower pots. A curious noise came from inside—an occasional click. Someone coughed. A gruff voice said, "Up it ten." "Ah, have a heart," said a whining voice, irritably.

Ellery decided that the object of the flower pots was to keep the neighbors from seeing in, while at the same time they permitted some air to circulate into the room through the slightly opened windows. However, he realized with satisfaction, it worked both ways. He would be able to peep between the pots with little chance of being seen by the people inside. Thin blue smoke was seeping out between the pots.

"Well, blast you, anyhow, R.M." That was the whining voice.

Someone laughed raucously—presumably R. M.

Click—click—click.

Ellery raised his head cautiously and put his eye to the gap between two pots.

At the far end of the room Count Brett was seated on a straight chair, apparently bored, and absently turning the pages of a magazine. Except for the table, the chairs on which the men were sitting, and a broken clothes tree leaning against the wall, the room was unfurnished. The bare floor was strewn with ashes, cigarette and cigar butts, and a dozen or so bottle caps. A high-watt bulb hanging at the end of a cord from the ceiling threw out a brilliant white light.

The men at the table were playing poker. The chips were unevenly divided. There were tall stacks of blues, whites, yellows, and reds before a big man with a long, sharp nose and a huge signet ring on one of his pudgy fingers. At his left sat a well-dressed but bleary-eyed man with no chips at all. Apparently he had been cleaned out. Beside him, with his back to Ellery, was a small man with thin, sandy hair and a bald spot at the back of his head. Ellery could not see his chips. To his left, in a loose tweed business suit, was another bleary-eyed man with his shirt open and his tie undone. He had a stack of white chips, a few blue ones, some reds, and a single yellow chip. The bleary-eyed men, although disheveled, were the only two who looked like gentlemen. Their clothes suggested that they were prosperous businessmen.

"Your deal, R. M." The man with his back to Ellery scooped up the cards and passed them to the man with the signet ring—and most of the chips.

Apparently R. M. was R. M. Smith, whose name was opposite the bell in the entry. He shuffled the pack three times and then dealt with the expertness of a professional gambler. Though the movement of his fingers was scarcely perceptible, the cards were flipped—sprayed, it seemed—to the four men still in the game.

"How about it, Ritter?" R. M. asked, rubbing his long nose with his thumb.

Ritter, the one with the bald spot, sitting with his back to Ellery, said, "Open for five."

There was a clatter as the players tossed chips on the table.

"How many, Ritter?"

Ritter held up one finger. R. M. flipped him a card.

"How about you, Robertson?" R. M. asked the man in tweeds. "You're shy, brother. Ante up."

"I'll take three." Robertson pushed five red chips toward the middle of the table.

R. M. flipped him three cards and then picked up his hand. Before looking at his cards, he studied Robertson's face. Robertson's foggy eyes blinked. R. M. glanced at his hand, discarded a card, and slipped the top card off the deck. Without looking at it, he slid it between the other four and left the hand face down before him.

"Ritter, wake up. I'm losing money while you snooze."

Ritter pushed out a stack of blue chips.

"Twenty," he said.

"Up you ten," Robertson said, straightening in his chair.

"And ten more," said R. M., after an apparent struggle.

The pile in the middle of the table was becoming impressive.

"Well, you pikers," Ritter said cheerfully, "it'll cost you a yellow to look." He pushed out a yellow chip.

"Say what is this?" Robertson said, "a millionaire's game?" He showed no reluctance, however, to chip in his last yellow counter.

"With your bank account, you should worry," R. M. said. "But I'm game; up another hundred." He tossed out two yellow chips.

"Come again," said Ritter, adding two more yellows to the pile.

"Boys will be boys," R. M. said.

Robertson frowned, counted his remaining chips, and pushed all except two reds into the pile.

"I'm calling," he said firmly.

"Calling, are you?" R. M. said, and laughed with self-assurance. "It'll cost any guy that wants to see my mitt three *C*'s."

There were six distinct clicks as the chips land-ed on the pile.

"Three and a couple more," Ritter said.

"Have a heart," said Robertson. "I'm cleaned."

"Here," said R. M. "I'll lend you five." He stacked up ten yellows and pushed them across the table.

The poor sucker, Ellery thought. So they were taking Robertson over with the old army game. R. M. and Ritter were working the squeeze. They could keep on raising until the cows came home. Either Robertson would finally have to drop out, having lost everything but his shirt, or else it was a crooked deal. Apparently the other bleary-eyed player, who was now nodding groggily, had al-ready been stripped.

That it was a crooked deal, plus a squeeze, Ellery was certain a few moments later. Robert-son called, Ritter raised two yellows, and Ritter dropped out. That meant that he didn't want to show his hand. Probably he held only two pairs, or had drawn for a flush and missed. Now Robertson could call and R. M. would have to show his hand. R. M. had dealt, and that, to a man who had all the earmarks of a cardsharp, was a distinct advantage.

"Put up or shut up, Robertson."

Robertson put up.

"Right. How do you like the looks of these babies?" he asked, laying down his cards. "Four aces!"

"Now, ain't that just too bad," R. M. said. " 'Nough to break a guy's heart. But I guess a straight flush licks you." He spread his cards into a fan and laid them on the table as his open laugh boomed.

Robertson swore. R. M. pushed back his chair and got up.

"Well, gentlemen, that ends the afternoon session. Anyone who wants revenge can show up tomorrow at two-thirty. With the last five, that makes seven hundred bucks, Robertson. Better luck next time."

Robertson got out his checkbook.

"Come to life, Fred," he said to the sunken man opposite him. "You owe Mr. Smith"—he paused a moment—"three hundred and fifty dollars."

"All ri', all ri'——" he said, and began to probe in his pockets. "Who's got a pen?"

No one spoke while the two checks were written out. Smith examined them carefully and put them in his wallet. Fred got up and, taking Robertson's arm, walked unsteadily toward the door.

"Better luck next time, boys," said R. M. Smith again lighting a cigar.

"And how!" Robertson said grimly.

As soon as the door closed behind the two men, Ritter said, grinning, "A thousand and fifty. Not so bad, not so bad."

R. M. took two fifty-dollar bills from his wallet and handed them to Ritter.

"Ah, come on, R. M.," Ritter whined, getting up.

He was shorter than Ellery had expected. Hollow-chested; a sallow complexion. His little eyes, protruding ears, and small nose gave him a mouselike appearance.

"Dry up," R. M. snapped. "I'm running this

show. Now, get out. Wait in the other room. I've got some business to talk over with Brett. Or better still, go dig up a couple more suckers."

"But, R. M.——"

"You heard me, flap-puss!"

Ritter shrugged and, muttering, left the room. Smith turned to Brett.

"What's the news at the Hollingsworth?" he asked, standing up.

He was over six feet, Ellery noticed—nearly as tall as Sergeant Velie.

Brett got up, slammed the magazine down on the chair, and came slowly toward the big man.

"I guess you ought to know, you dirty double-crosser."

Gone was the count's suave manner. Gone was his insolence and his foreign accent

R. M.'s face had turned gray.

"You talk like that and I'll slap you down, runt." He stepped toward Brett threateningly. "What do you mean?"

Brett backed away, cringing.

"Well, if you didn't pull a fast one, who did?"

"Did what?"

"Cobb's dead."

"Dead! Did you say, 'Dead'?"

"Yeah. Murdered."

R. M. gaped at him, speechless.

CHAPTER VIII

Vanishing Suspects

Ellery Queen twisted himself into a more comfortable position and listened.

"Gordon Cobb was murdered?" he heard Smith ask finally, in little more than a whisper.

"He was murdered on the day he arrived," Brett said, sullenly.

Smith scowled and looked suspiciously at Brett.

"He was bumped off two days ago, and you didn't tell me?"

"Now, cut that," Brett said. "I didn't know until a while ago. The poker game had started when I got here. I couldn't talk until the suckers left, could I? Cobb was strangled and locked in a trunk. Someone arranged for the trunk to be expressed to Chicago. So I guess whoever conked him didn't get what he was after."

"How do you figure that?" Smith asked.

"If he had, he'd have beat it without bothering to pack Cobb in the trunk. He did that because he didn't want the police around before he had a chance to search the place again. He was playing for time. That's why he arranged to have the trunk expressed."

Smith twisted the signet ring on his finger.

"What was that you told me about some Japs or someone being on the *Manchuria?*"

"No Japs, but there's plenty that's screwy about the set-up. Sorry about the crack I made, R. M."

Smith's anger flared again.

"Get it through your noggin that I don't go in for killing, and I won't stand for it from anyone on my payroll. Where were you that day?"

"You know where I was. I was watching from the door of my penthouse for him to go out. I was going to slip in from the terrace, just as you told me to. But he never went out. So drop your insinuations. Somebody beat us to it. But he didn't get away with the swag. So what? We've got to use our brains."

"Why do you think there's something screwy about the set-up?" Smith asked.

Brett frowned.

"Well, first, Cobb's steward on the boat is bellhopping at the Hollingsworth. Maybe that isn't screwy! Then the jane I told you about, Olga Otero, is stopping there, too. Well, in Hong Kong she was seeing a lot of a certain Japanese. What I figure is that he got onto Cobb's sailing on the *Manchuria,* just about the time I did. He came to the hotel at the last moment with a ticket for her. It's like pulling hen's teeth to get passage from China to the U.S.A. There's a waiting list a mile long. It takes connections to pull one like that. Then on the boat Otero and Cobb were as palsy as lovebirds."

"If you'd had any sense you'd have gotten palsy yourself."

Brett shook his head.

"No good doing anything until the stuff passed the customs. I was doing the count act. I made a play for Otero to get the dope on Cobb's plans. But did she tell me she was going to stop at the Hollingsworth? She did not, the——!"

"Did Cobb declare the stuff at the customs?" Smith growled.

"Don't make me laugh. Does a smuggler put it down in writing?"

"Chuck it," Smith said. "Cobb wasn't a smuggler. He may have put it over on you by making two declarations. Or he may have shipped it from 'Frisco to New York in bond. They don't come any smarter than Cobb. He outsmarted you in spite of your warning, Brett, but I guess he didn't outsmart someone else." Smith took out a cigar. He wet it with his tongue and jabbed the end into the corner of his mouth. "The first thing to settle is what you're to do now. You can't go back to the Hollingsworth. If the cops pick you up, and they're sure to, they'll find out that you're Arkie Brett, the confidence man, not a Count La de Da in spite of that fancy talk of yours."

"You're darn tootin' I'm not going back," Brett said heartily.

"You send the hotel a wire saying that you'll be out of town for a couple of days."

"How about my things?"

"I'll have Ritter pick them up when the time comes. As long as we keep your apartment we can get into Cobb's. In the meantime we'll keep an eye on your bellhop. What's his name?"

"Sanders."

"On Sanders and the Otero dame. One or both of them is trying to cut in on our game."

"And others, maybe," Brett suggested. "If the Japs knew, and they must have, you can count on their having plenty of agents on the job."

"Never mind about the Japs," Smith said irritably. "Your trip to China cost a load of dough —what with all that flying. It's our business to get there ahead of whoever else is in on this deal. They found out, and that's that. If the bellhop or the Otero suddenly pulls a fade-out, we'll know who's got away with the stuff. I'll have some of the boys on their tails. You'll have to lay low."

"You're mighty worried about me, R. M., aren't you?" Brett said with sarcasm. "If I get picked up, the cops'll know I'm working for R. M. Smith, eh?"

"Shut your face," Smith snapped at him. "Come on, let's get out of here."

Brett had put his hand on the door, when it opened suddenly, and Ritter came in.

"Say, Chief," he said, "I was halfway to Times Square when suddenly I gets a brainstorm."

"Oh, yeah?" Smith looked at him suspiciously.

"If there's something up at the Hollingsworth, why shouldn't I hang around there? It's as good a place as any to pick up a couple of customers, and I could keep my eye peeled."

"There's been a murder at the Hollingsworth. Do you want to stick your neck out? Keep away from there, sap!"

Ellery Queen started to back away toward the ladder, and then hesitated. It was important to get to the street before the others. It was important, too, to know where Brett was going to hide out. But on the other hand, Ellery had come to an interesting conclusion about Ritter.

"But, Chief——" Ritter began.

"Shut up. Can't you see I'm thinking?" Smith's gaze was fixed on the ceiling.

"It's not a bad idea, R. M.," Brett suggested.

Smith looked at Ritter.

"Call me at the Swiftfield in a half hour and I'll give you orders."

"O.K., Chief." Ritter stood watching the others leave.

After a minute or two he took a wad of chewing gum from his mouth and stuffed it in the keyhole of the door.

So I was right, Ellery thought. Ritter had been in the other room listening at the keyhole, which Smith probably had plugged up as a precaution against such curiosity on the part of his underlings. Then when Smith and Brett suddenly started to leave, Ritter had nearly been caught. He had saved himself by boldly walking in. Even Ritter was trying to work in on the racket! Though he didn't know exactly what it was, he saw that it was obviously a big deal.

Ritter went from the door to the table and began to sort and stack the chips. Suddenly he stopped and picked up the pack of cards. He spread them out face down and studied them carefully. After a moment or two he scooped them up and put them into his pocket.

Ellery Queen slithered backward to the ladder. In the court he picked up the ashcan and carried it back to the passage. Smith and Brett were not in sight when he reached the street. He hailed a cab.

"To the Hotel Swiftfield," he said to the driver. "And step on it!"

Ellery was reading a paper in the lobby of

the Swiftfield on West Twenty-seventh Street when Smith and Brett came through the revolving door. He held the paper spread out wide before his face until they were in the elevator. Then he got up and strolled over to the desk.

"Say, Bud," he said to the clerk, "I'm working for U.P. Wasn't that Gabriel McCann who just registered?"

"Who's Gabriel McCann?"

"You know—the movie actor."

The clerk looked interested.

"Well, maybe. Sometimes they don't use their screen names. This guy registered as T. P. Pringle."

"Maybe I'm wrong," Ellery said, frowning, "but it sure looked like him."

It was eight o'clock when Ellery got out his latchkey to open the door of the Queen apartment on West Eighty-seventh Street. As he put the key into the lock and started to turn the knob the door was jerked open from the inside.

Annie, the Queens' gray-haired Irish maid, cook, and factotum, ruler of the household, confronted him.

"And it's a fine how-do-you-do, it is, your coming home late for dinner again," she said, arms akimbo.

"Oh, I ate out, Annie," Ellery said blithely.

"So ye did, did you? And you didn't have a nickel to phone you wouldn't be home. It's a fine how-do-you-do, it is. As if I didn't have me hands full with your dad and his carryings on."

"What's the matter with Dad?" Ellery closed the door.

"He's in a state, he is—abusin' the poor sergeant something awful."

"Poor little Velie," Ellery murmured sympathetically. "What's the old ox done now?"

"Old ox! The sergeant's a cherub, he is. And the inspector abusin' him!"

Ellery grinned.

"Hope I'm in time for the knockout. Here's a present for you, Annie." He handed her his hat, laughing.

Annie slapped it down on the hall table and stalked off down the hall toward the kitchen. Ellery went into the living room.

Inspector Queen, his gray hair ruffled, was angrily blowing through his mustache. Standing before Sergeant Velie, who cowered in an easy chair, he was pointing a forefinger as though it were the barrel of a pistol. As Ellery came in, he turned from his victim and glared.

"So it's you, Ellery!"

"Were you expecting the commissioner?" Ellery asked cheerfully.

"Hang the commissioner!" The inspector screwed up his face at the very thought of that potentate. "Do you know what this cluck has done?" The finger was again leveled at Velie.

"No, I don't," Ellery shook his head. "But you can generally count on his doing something fairly unexpected."

The sergeant was spiritually in no condition to show resentment.

"He's let every one of them get away—every blasted one of them!"

"Of whom?"

"Of whom! What do you mean, of whom?" A blast of air flared out the inspector's whiskers. "The bellboy, Sanders—gone! That bogus Count Brett—skipped. The Otero woman's cleared out of the hotel, bag and baggage. No forwarding address. And we haven't been able to locate Walsh. He's probably on the lam too."

Ellery yawned.

"I wouldn't worry about Walsh's pulling a fade-out, Dad. He's probably attending to some personal business. You can get in touch with him in the morning. So Brett wired the Hollingsworth that he would be out of town for a few days, did he?"

Inspector Queen squinted his eyes at Ellery.

"How did you know that?"

"I heard someone say that he was going to."

"Look here, Ellery," the inspector said, still squinting. "I thought you said you were quitting the case—walking out on me. What have *you* been up to?"

"I've quit. I quit a couple of hours ago. I have to get some work done, don't I? But I don't like to be followed."

"What's that? I didn't have you tailed."

"No, that was Brett's bright idea. He's registered as T. P. Pringle at the Swiftfield."

Velie jumped up from his chair. His big hands grabbed Ellery's shoulders.

"Ellery, if you're kidding, I'll monopolize you!"

"Now, now," said Ellery, "you two have got yourselves all in a dither. Calm down. Take a seat, Dad. Light up your favorite briar—the one that smells like smoldering rubber—and I'll tell you all about it."

CHAPTER IX

JIM SANDERS

THE FOLLOWING morning Ellery Queen awakened resolved to have nothing whatever to do with the mystery of the murder of Gordon Cobb. He arrived at his office before Nikki Porter, determined to write at least two chapters that day to make up for lost time. But as he sat at his desk, certain phases of the Cobb case kept tormenting him.

For instance, he asked himself, how account for there having been no Chinese passenger on the *Manchuria*—as the San Francisco police had reported to his father? Had either Olga Otero or Sanders got away with whatever they all were after before Smith, Brett and Company had got into action? The inspector had had reports on all of them as well as on Harry Walsh.

Walsh's record held nothing to invite suspicion. Some years before, he had been a fight promotor. Some of his promotions looked a bit shady, but there was nothing you could pin down.

Then he had become a vaudeville booking agent until vaudeville sang its swan song. More recently he had been acting as manager and agent for foreign artists, concert singers, violinists, and pianists as well as a ballet or two. Cobb and Walsh were old friends. Walsh had got Cobb's first Chinese bookings for him about twenty years ago.

But R. M. Smith's reputation was unsavory, to put it mildly. He had made his début on the police records as an international cardsharp, working the transatlantic liners. When he became too well known to the steamship companies, he gave up this profession and got mixed up in a bucket shop scandal in Wall Street. Somehow he had squirmed out of that, letting his front men take the rap. Then he'd gone back to cardsharping, using Brett, Ritter, and others as decoys for rich out-of-town businessmen. They were careful to avoid the local gentry, but picked up likely acquaintances in the better hotels.

Brett and Ritter were confidence men. Ritter had once been a stage magician, billed as THE INGENIOUS CORRI. Perhaps that——

"Oh, Ellery!"

Ellery Queen's train of thought was snapped. Nikki came in.

Ellery looked at his watch pointedly.

"Only a half hour late," he said. "What's the matter? Wasn't the bed comfortable?"

"As a matter of fact, I *couldn't* sleep. So skip the sarcasm." She sank onto a chair. "What a night!"

"Well, what was the matter with the night?" He put down his pencil on the blank pad and leaned back. "*I* slept like a top."

"First of all, Mr. Walsh came to see Sheila. He talked and talked. Then——"

"What did he want?"

Nikki sighed.

"I think he's getting ready to make a play for Sheila. She's awfully attractive, I noticed you noticed, and I suppose she'll be rich, now."

"What did he talk about?"

"Did you follow the count, Ellery? Where did he go?"

"To the Hotel Swiftfield. What did Walsh talk about?"

"Oh, about Mr. Cobb's affairs. He said he thought he ought to turn everything over to Sheila now, or pretty soon. Mr. Cobb had given him power of attorney, but it seems that it's void, now. After her father's death, you see. He said that if Sheila would give him a note to the hotel, he'd go there and pack up Mr. Cobb's things. He was awfully thoughtful and nice. He knew she'd hate to."

"So that's why you couldn't sleep—because he was so nice."

Nikki yawned.

"No, we didn't get to bed until all hours. Who do you suppose descended on us next? That bell-boy! Jimmy Sanders, his name is. And he isn't a bellboy at all. Did you ever? He's awfully attractive in his street clothes."

"Business clothes."

She yawned again.

"No, street clothes. You'd call his uniform business clothes."

"Skip it. What did he want? And what is he, if he isn't a bellhop?"

Nikki shook her head, puzzled.

"I don't know. He didn't say. He just said that he wasn't a bellboy."

"Well, what was he doing at Sheila's?"

"Oh, it's *Sheila* already, is it? Well, he's fallen for her, too. His eyes get as big as saucers when he looks at her. Some girls get all the breaks."

"Will you tell me what he went to see her about?" Ellery asked patiently.

"He wanted to help her, of course. Help her find out who murdered her father."

"If he wanted to help, why did he run away? Why didn't he go to the police?"

"Oh, he won't have anything to do with the police. He said they'd jinx everything. He wants to free-lance it." She beamed suddenly. "Yes, that's what he said he was! A free-lance. Now you know."

Ellery began to feel a mild irritation. Whenever Nikki wanted to annoy him she got kittenish.

"Did he tell Sheila where she could reach him?"

"No. He was afraid the police might get it out of her. Jimmy Sanders knows all about you, Ellery. He thinks you're wonderful. Isn't it grand to be famous? He said he'd keep in touch with Sheila."

Ellery scowled.

"And just how does he plan to help her?"

"He says he suspects certain people," Nikki said mysteriously. "He knows a lot that he can't tell—not yet. He wanted to borrow Sheila's key."

"Her key? What key?"

"To the penthouse, of course. What key would he want to borrow? Don't be tedious."

"What did he want it for?"

"To look for a clue, naturally. You *are* stupid this morning, Ellery."

Ellery suddenly sat up straight.

"Did she give it to him?"

"No, she thanked him, but said that she had complete confidence in you, that you were handling this case. She gave me the key to give to you."

Ellery managed to keep from exploding.

"I'm not having anything to do with the case. Will you please get that through your head? And trot yourself right over to the typewriter. I'm——"

"But, Ellery, I couldn't possibly do any work today. Do you think with Sheila——? Do you think for one minute that I'd stay here and type when——? Well, if you're not going to help, then I have to work on the case alone. And——"

The door to the private office opened, and a young man stood in the doorway.

Ellery started. Definitely there was something familiar about him, but what? Oh, of course. Sanders!

Sanders took off his hat. In his well-cut and freshly pressed worsted suit, nothing that suggested the former bellboy remained.

"Sorry," he said. "I knocked several times, but no one seemed to hear."

"Why, Mr. Sanders!" Nikki said in surprise. "No wonder we didn't hear. Ellery, you shouldn't shout so."

"Good morning, Miss Porter. I was hoping you'd be here. How's Miss Cobb?"

"She's feeling pretty low, naturally. Ellery, you remember Mr. Sanders."

Ellery Queen nodded.

"How are you, Mr. Queen?" Sanders reached his hand across the desk. "I didn't realize yesterday that you were the famous mystery writer. I want to put a proposition to you. It's right up your alley."

"Suppose you tell me who you are first."

"Jim Sanders, the name is," the other replied.

"Means nothing to me."

Sanders grinned ruefully.

"I'm not a by-liner, I have to admit—not yet. I work for the New York *Post-Dispatch*. I did until yesterday, that is. The editor canned me." He grinned again. "That's what editors are for— to shout at people, push a blue pencil, and fire you."

"What were you fired for?"

"For using my initiative. 'Man,' the editor says, 'use your initiative. You won't get to first base unless you use your own initiative.' I use it. He fires me. That's an editor."

Ellery chuckled.

"Maybe his idea of initiative isn't the same as yours."

"So it seems. There's nothing relative about being fired, though. He was quite definite. However, I've still got thirty-five bucks, so I'm neither down nor out."

"Congratulations. Excuse me a moment."

Ellery got up and, going into the outer office, closed the door after him.

In a few moments he returned.

"Well," he said, sitting down at his desk, "it seems that you are Jim Sanders, that you were a reporter for the P.-D. until yesterday, and that you just returned from China."

"It more than seems, Mr. Queen. It's a fact."

"From the tone of your editor's voice," Ellery said mildly, "I gather you didn't see eye to eye on the meaning of initiative. He says you came back from China with no authority and contrary to orders."

"Yes, that's right."

"Well, what's your proposition?"

Sanders looked speculatively at him for a moment, and then spoke deliberately.

"I've got some dope on the Cobb murder, important dope. I'll swap it with you for the dope you've got, on one condition."

"Namely?"

"That it isn't passed on to the police."

Ellery Queen looked at him coldly.

"If you know anything that will throw light on the murder of Gordon Cobb, you better hie yourself over to headquarters in a hurry. If you think I'm going to hold any information back from the inspector, you may as well get out before I throw you out."

"Now, don't get riled, Mr. Queen. I'm not proposing anything of the sort. I know that you shoot square. So do I. And I'm not a fool. News is my business, and I ought to know my business by this time. I'm going to get the murderer of Gordon Cobb if it's my last act on earth. When I'm ready, everything I've got goes to the police —and my paper. It'll be my scoop. See? They'll up me to a couple of hundred a week and beg me to come back. Now, do I tell my story—confidentially—or don't I? Incidentally, I've been thrown out of lots better offices than yours, Mr. Queen."

There was something engaging about Sanders's breeziness and candor. Ellery Queen turned round in his swivel chair to look out the window.

After a moment he said, "I'll make you a counter-proposal. Tell me your story. If I think it's straight—and I'm to be sole judge—I'll give you a letter to my father and a guarantee that what you tell me or him won't be given to any other reporter or paper until the case breaks. And I'll guarantee that you'll be in on it when it does."

"Fair enough. Shake." Again Sanders reached across the desk and shook Ellery's hand.

"O.K., Mr. Queen, here goes. Three years ago my paper sent me to China to cover the war. I got to know the ropes—and they're plenty to learn! A couple of months ago I got wind of something big. Big's too small a word for it. Never mind how I got onto it. There are sources of information a news-hound wouldn't spill if you put him on the rack.

"Tuan Yen-sung is one of the biggest shots in China. He's one of the big financial powers backing the government. All right. Do you know Chinatown, either here or in San Francisco?"

Ellery nodded.

"Passably well."

"Ever hear of Li Soo?"

"I know he's one of the most important and influential Chinese in this country."

"O.K. Well, Li Soo's a close friend of Tuan Yen-sung. Now get this. Tuan begins having secret conferences with Chinese big mucks. What they were about, frankly, I don't know. But I'm supposed to use my initiative, so I'm interested. For a time my war cables to the paper are pretty skimpy. The ed gets a bit peevish. But what can I do? If I cable about what I think's brewing, my life isn't worth a plug without a dime around it. Besides, the cable wouldn't get through. Then, mysteriously, out of nowhere, Li Soo shows up in Hong Kong. I see him go into Tuan's. He doesn't come out. I cable the paper to find out what's up. I have to be cagey. I just say, 'Advise whereabouts of Li Soo.' The ed cables back, 'Li in New York. No story received three days.' Go climb a tree, I say. Li Soo's in Hong Kong. I saw him with my own eyes. I keep on covering Tuan's. There's a final meeting of potentates, and Gordon Cobb's sent for. I find out Cobb's sailing the next day on the *Manchuria.* The *Manchuria's* a U. S. boat. She's supposed to pick up passengers at Yokohama, but at the last moment she's ordered to proceed directly to San Francisco. Maybe you don't know it, but Gordon Cobb is one of the few foreigners who was ever in the confidence of the Chinese big shots. He could speak the language like a native, and could act like one—their manners and courtesy, I mean. And he understood their humor. Well, a blind man could see what was up.

"A newspaperman in China these days needs contacts and friends. I'd made plenty. I'd done a couple of good turns for the captain of the *Manchuria.* He takes me on as a steward.

"Well, I've got my neck out a porthole when who do I see come aboard the third-class gangway but Li Soo, dressed as a coolie. Li Soo, a *coolie.* One of the richest Chinese in America! Whether or not he got off again, I don't know. I never saw him after that. I spotted Cobb coming up the first-class gangway and I beat it for his cabin.

"He had two bags. The one he brought to the

Hollingsworth, and another. I'll come back to that in a minute. The trunk was put in the hold. *The ship sailed two hours late.* Underscore that. I got a word in with the captain on the fourth day out. He told me that the boat had been held at the request of the Japanese consul, to wait for a lady passenger named Otero. One of the ship's officers had to move out of his quarters so she could have a cabin. Right off—the first time Cobb went on deck, that is—she starts to make a play for him—and she's sure vaseline on the eyes!

"Well, now, about that bag. It was a cowhide case about four feet long, three feet broad, and two deep. Cobb carried it to his cabin himself. He didn't let it out of his sight for a second until it finally disappeared."

"Disappeared?" Ellery straightened up. "What do you mean?"

"Vanished. Cobb stayed in his cabin for two days. He had all his meals there. On the morning of the third day, when I took in his breakfast, he'd already gone above. The bag was gone.

"One day I said, 'Mr. Cobb, didn't you have

another bag?' 'Oh, sure,' he said. 'I had the purser send it down to the hold.'

"And that, Mr. Queen, was a lie. Well, that's
my story. What's the verdict?"

"You win, Sanders," Ellery said. "You win
hands down."

CHAPTER X

Lois Ling

ELLERY called his father at headquarters as soon as Sanders had left his office with a letter to the inspector.

"Dad," he said, "the bellhop, Sanders, is on his way downtown to see you. He's got a tall tale to tell you. He's a smart boy. Too smart, maybe. If he's collecting Chinese souvenirs, there's something more valuable than the missing jade necklace. Don't tell him that you're wiring the Coast to find out if there was a Chinese among the crew." After a pause, Ellery said, "Well, it's a trick he missed. I hope you don't, too. Remember my telling you that there had to be a Chinese in the picture? So long, Dad!"

As he hung up, Nikki said, "Ellery, are you going ahead with the case? You will, won't you?"

"I don't even want to talk about it. I'm a taxpayer. Taxes pay for the police. That's final, Nikki. I don't want to argue. Get to work."

To his surprise, she smiled and said, "All

right." Leaving the door open, she went to her desk in the outer office.

In a moment the keys started clicking. Ellery got up and closed the door. Back at his desk, he wrote "CHAPTER VIII, THE WEAPON," at the top of the pad. Now he would get on with the *Braun Murder Mystery*. He had written only a few paragraphs when a sound made him look up.

"Ellery."

Nikki was in the doorway.

"What is it, now?"

"Be a lamb and get me a coke."

"Why don't you skip down to the drugstore?"

"I don't want to waste the time, Ellery. Please. Be a lamb."

When Ellery returned five minutes later, carrying a bottle of Coca-Cola with two straws protruding from its neck, he was surprised to find the door of his suite locked. As he fished for his key, he decided that Nikki had stepped out for a minute. He opened the door and frowned. Not only had Nikki gone, but she had closed up the typewriter desk and put away the manuscript.

Scowling, he went into his office. On his desk was a typewritten note. He picked it up.

Ellery—I had to get you out so that I could borrow your gadget in the bottom drawer. Since you're so mean about it, I'll have to carry on alone. I was starting to tell you when Mr. Sanders came in that someone tried to get into Sheila's apartment from the fire escape last night. Fortunately she woke up and that frightened him away. So I'm borrowing your gadget.

NIKKI

P.S.—You can drink the coke yourself. I don't mind.

Ellery jerked open the bottom drawer. His .32 automatic pistol was gone. For some time he sat thinking, and the more he thought the angrier he became. He waited a half hour and then called Sheila's apartment. Sheila answered.

No, she said, Nikki wasn't there. Nikki had said nothing about bringing a gun home. Nikki had told her that she and Ellery Queen were going back to the penthouse to look for clues.

Ellery hung up, more incensed than ever. Nikki knew nothing about guns. She would probably hurt herself—more likely, someone else.

Would she have gone to the penthouse alone?
Sheila had given her the key! Of course there
was no clue to be found there. The inspector had
ordered all Cobb's personal belongings removed
to headquarters for minute examination. There
wouldn't even be a policeman on guard there.
But the murderer wouldn't know about the re-
moval. The murderer might return and——

The phone rang.

"Hello, hello," Ellery said irritably.

He recognized Nikki's voice. She was whis-
pering so softly that he could scarcely hear her.
Some of the words were lost entirely.

"—Ellery. It's me. I'm—Mr. Cobb's penthouse
—Chinese—your Chinese."

A horrible rattling sound came over the wire.

"Help! Help!" she screamed.

The line was disconnected.

Frantically Ellery thumbed the pages of the
phone book. Hotel—Hotel—Hotel Hermitage
—Hilmont—Holley—Hollingsworth. PL-9-9000.

Busy! All the lines busy?

He hung up and dialed operator.

"Operator get me PL-9-9000. Quick."

"Just a moment, please—sorry, the line's busy."

"Operator—listen! That's the Hollingsworth. Someone's being murdered there. Connect me at once."

"I'll connect you with the supervisor, sir. Just a moment, please," the operator said with the same toneless voice she had used to tell him the line was busy.

Sweat broke out on Ellery's forehead.

"Hotel Hollingsworth, good morning."

"There's your party, sir. Thank you."

"Hello, a girl's being murdered in penthouse 17A. Send someone up at once."

"Beg pardon, sir?"

"Listen, will you? *A girl's being murdered in 17A!* Get someone up there!"

"Heavens!"

The line was disconnected.

Ellery dialed.

S—P—7—3—1—0—0.

"Inspector Queen, quick."

"Hello."

"Dad!"

"Hello, son. That you again? Sanders——"

"Dad, Nikki's being murdered in the Cobb penthouse."

"Huh?"

"Quick, Dad, quick."

He hung up and dashed for the elevators.

Twelve minutes later Ellery tore across the hall on the seventeenth floor of the Hollingsworth. The door to 17A was ajar. He pushed it open and stopped dead on the threshold.

He gaped at Nikki, who was sitting with his gun on her lap. Beside her stood Parkman, the manager. Frowning, he looked like a disgruntled floorwalker. Opposite Nikki was an almond-eyed Chinese girl. She was young, pretty, and smartly dressed in American clothes. Only her eyes showed annoyance. Otherwise her face was inscrutable.

"What's happened, Nikki?"

Parkman answered for her.

"Someone called the hotel and reported that a girl was being murdered in this apartment. I came up with the house detective. I found this young lady"—he indicated Nikki—"pointing a pistol at this young lady. She said she'd shoot anyone that tried to take it away from her before you arrived, Mr. Queen."

Ellery Queen went to Nikki, took the automatic, and slipped it into his pocket.

A man with a big nose and big hands and feet came slouching out of Cobb's bedroom.

"I can't see anything's been touched," he said to Parkman.

Parkman was introducing the house detective to Ellery when Inspector Queen, followed by Sergeant Velie, stalked into the room.

The inspector glanced at the others and turned to Ellery.

"Well," he snapped, "what's the meaning of the convention?"

Ellery shrugged.

"The meeting was called by Miss Porter. Ask her about it."

Suddenly the center of attention, Nikki flushed.

"I—I—" she stammered, and then managed to compose herself. "Ellery refused to have anything to do with the case, so I had to carry on alone. Miss Cobb gave me the key. I came here to look around. I hadn't been here more than a minute or two when there was a knock at the

door. I opened it, and there stood this person."
She glanced pleadingly at Ellery. "You said there
was a Chinese at the bottom of this. Well, she's
the blackmailer."

"Huh? What's this? Blackmailer? What
blackmailer?" The inspector looked bewildered.

"The person who was blackmailing Mr. Cobb.
She had one of the cards in her hand when I
pointed the gun at her."

"Gun?" the inspector asked incredulously.
"What gun?"

"The gun Ellery loaned me. He has it now."

The inspector dazedly ran his fingers through
his gray hair and scowled at Ellery.

"You lent her a gun?" he demanded.

"The way a bank president lends ten thousand bucks to the teller who leaves during the
night."

Nikki decided to change the subject.

"Look. She had this in her hand. It's one of
the black hand cards." She handed the inspector
a card similar to those previously addressed to
Gordon Cobb.

Looking at the broad handprinting, he read,

"APPOINTED PLACE, RAT." He turned to the Chinese girl.

"Who are you?"

"I am Lois Ling," she said in a low voice.

"How long have you been in this country?"

"I was born here. I'm an American."

The intonation of her voice tended to confirm both statements. Her New York accent with its Park Avenue inflection was a little disconcerting, coming from one so obviously Oriental. The smart crêpe dress of apple-green, the high-heeled shoes that exposed the tips of two toes, the rouged cheeks, the carefully waved black hair, all belied her Chinese ancestry.

"Why did you attack Miss Porter?" Inspector Queen asked.

The almond eyes became wider.

"I didn't attack anyone. This young lady"—she nodded toward Nikki—"is trying to frame me. She pointed a pistol at me. She said she'd shoot me if I didn't do as she said. She made me come in here. Then she telephoned someone. She whispered into the phone and then——"

"I—I had to use a subterfuge," Nikki interrupted quickly. "I knew Ellery wouldn't come unless—unless—well, unless I used a subterfuge."

Ellery snorted.

"Subterfuge! She yelled bloody murder."

The inspector blew through his whiskers.

"Nikki, how many times do I have to tell you to keep out of police affairs? The downright impudence of your——"

"Now, Inspector," Nikki protested innocently. "I didn't phone *you* that I was being attacked, and I didn't say so to Ellery. How can I help it if he calls you up and says that——"

"Quiet," the inspector said gruffly. The futility of arguing with Nikki was, alas, an unchangeable fact. He turned back to Miss Ling. "What is the meaning of this card?" he asked, tapping it.

"I haven't any idea."

"Then, what were you doing with it?"

"Nothing. I picked it up from the floor outside the door."

The inspector was skeptical.

"What did you come here for?"

"I came to see Mr. Cobb, of course."

"Who told you that you'd find him here?"

"He did."

The inspector started.

"When?"

"He telephoned me as soon as he arrived. He asked me to come at once."

"When was that?"

"Three days ago."

"Why didn't you come then?" Queen queried.

"I did. But he wasn't in. So I waited to hear from him. But he never called. So I came back today."

"What did he want to see you about?"

"A confidential matter."

"What confidential matter? Come, speak up."

"A confidential matter that does not concern you in the least," she said quietly but firmly, with complete self-assurance.

The inspector squinted, contriving for an instant to look Chinese himself.

"Anything that concerns Mr. Cobb concerns me very much indeed."

Lois Ling shrugged and looked away.

"Miss Ling, you know that Mr. Cobb is dead?"

Her head jerked round. She stared at him.

"Mr. Cobb was murdered, Miss Ling, shortly after he telephoned you."

She gasped and jumped up from her chair.

"Murdered! Oh, No!" As if suddenly weak, she sank back into the chair. After a moment she looked up at the inspector and said, "But there was nothing about his death in the papers."

"No, we saw that the story didn't get out."

Lois Ling was puzzled.

"May I ask who you are?" she asked abruptly.

Inspector Queen introduced himself.

"I must talk with you privately, at once," she said, her agitation returning.

The inspector dismissed Parkman and the house detective and then turned to Nikki.

"You can wait out on the terrace," he said.

"But, Inspector——" Nikki began to protest.

"Run along," he said irritably, and turned to the sergeant. "Go along with her, Velie. See if you can keep her out of mischief."

Velie caught Nikki's elbow and dragged her off.

"This is my son, Ellery," the inspector explained, sitting down opposite Lois Ling. "Now, tell me, Miss Ling, have you any idea why anyone should want to murder Gordon Cobb?"

"Inspector Queen, Mr. Cobb had millions of dollars' worth of jewels in his possession! Are they safe?"

The inspector's bushy eyebrows shot up.

"Millions in jewels, you say? *Millions?*"

"Yes, jewelry that was absolutely priceless."

"Mr. Cobb declared a jade necklace." The inspector reached in his pocket. "I called the customs at San Francisco for a description of it. Here," he said, reading from a notebook, " 'necklace of twenty-six filigreed pink jade discs, uniform in size, and a large pendant also of pink jade, carved with Chinese characters.' Of course, jade can be very valuable but——"

"No, no," the girl interrupted impatiently, "he was bringing to this country an absolutely priceless collection of Chinese heirlooms. Poor Mr. Cobb. He has given his life for China. The Chinese loved him. We all loved him. And now they've murdered him. They have stolen our treasure." Her Oriental impassivity was gone. She sat tense, her fingers clenched, staring furiously down at the rose-taupe rug. "But they shan't beat us," she murmured. "They shan't beat us." Suddenly she looked up at the inspector. "We must be quick. They mustn't get out of the country. Oh they're clever—clever and cruel . . . . You *will* help us, won't you, Inspector Queen?"

"You'd better tell me all about it, Miss Ling," he said, quietly.

"Yes, I shall tell you. I shall tell you all I know." Her gaze seemed to be penetrating incredible distances, to pass one imaginary horizon after another, until finally it reached a land on the other side of the earth.

CHAPTER XI

THE JADE NECKLACE

THERE COULD be no question, Ellery realized, about Lois Ling's sincerity, her love of the land of her ancestors, and her fervent desire to help them in their time of trial. Vividly she described the struggle of the Chinese against the invader, their hardships and suffering from famine and disease, their heroic resistance, and faith in ultimate victory. The Chinese in America, she told the inspector, had organized to give all possible help to lessen the suffering of their people in the homeland. But their resources were pitifully limited, as were the funds of the Chinese government.

The leader of the Support-for-China movement in this country was Li Soo, she said. A few months ago, when the funds of the organization had become exhausted, Li Soo had devised a great plan for the shipment of medical supplies to Rangoon and thence over the Burma Road to the interior of China. To carry out the plan, millions of dollars were needed, but millions of lives would be saved by preventing the spread of plague and famine, and Li Soo had thought of a way to raise the millions. He had sent an emissary to Tuan Yen-sung, his friend and one of the great powers in China. Tuan had immediately approved the plan and taken action. He called together the richest and most influential of the Chinese businessmen. They had been commissioned to collect the gems and jewelry that had for centuries been in the possession of the great families.

Then Li Soo disappeared. It was believed that he himself had gone to China. The whole scheme had to be carried out with the utmost secrecy. The enemy would stop at nothing to prevent the transfer of the fabulous jewels to this country, where they were to be converted into cash to purchase supplies to be shipped to the suffering people of China.

Gordon Cobb was entrusted with this important mission. He was to bring the jewels to America. In the meantime, funds had been raised here to pay the customs duties. Enough money was already in the bank to cover them. It was merely necessary for Mr. Cobb to endorse the customs receipt over to the Support-for-China Society, of which Lois Ling was the treasurer. To outwit the enemy, everything up to that point was to be handled by Gordon Cobb. Li Soo, wherever he was, would remain in hiding until the jewels were actually sold.

When Lois Ling finished her story, the inspector got up and for a few moments restlessly paced the room. Finally he stopped and looked at her as though he were wondering how much of what she had said he could believe.

"Miss Ling," he announced, "you have to come down to headquarters. I'm sorry, but we'll have to detain you until we've checked up on you. I believe you've been telling me the truth—as far as you know it. But there are certain things that don't quite jibe. For instance, there isn't any customs receipt, because Mr. Cobb didn't declare any jewelry besides the necklace I mentioned."

Lois Ling got up.

"Are you implying that we smuggled the jewels into the country?"

"I'm implying nothing," he said. "I'm stating a fact."

"Of course," Ellery said, "there's the possibility

that he smuggled them in on his own account, with the idea of stealing them. But I don't think so, as they aren't all that's missing."

Lois Ling turned quickly to Ellery.

"Mr. Cobb was neither a smuggler nor a thief," she said firmly, and then looked at the inspector. "I'll go with you gladly to headquarters, Inspector Queen. The jewels must be recovered. I'm sorry, desperately sorry, that Mr. Cobb has been killed. His life was sacrificed for China. But there are thousands of other lives at stake. You will get the jewels back, won't you?"

"I'll do everything in my power, of course, Miss Ling. Who can substantiate your story?"

"My father and the heads of the Support-for-China Society."

Ellery started for the terrace.

"Where you off to, son?" the inspector called after him.

He wheeled round.

"I'm going to park Nikki at Miss Cobb's. Then I'm going to work."

"Look here, El, can't you lay off your writing for a few days and——?"

"Sure, Dad, that's what I meant. I'm going to work for China."

"Oh, Ellery," Nikki said in the taxicab after he had outlined Lois Ling's story to her, "I can't tell you how glad I am that you're going to work on the case. But why the sudden change of mind?"

"Solving a murder mystery's one thing," he said. "Helping to save thousands of lives is another." As the cab turned onto Fourth Street, he leaned forward and touched the driver's shoulder. "It's the second red brick house on the right, near the end of the block." Suddenly he gripped the man's shoulder. "Stop here. Draw up to the curb."

"What's the matter?" Nikki asked as Ellery quickly sat back.

"Olga Otero's been calling on Sheila. She just came out."

Nikki saw the lithe figure of a woman in black going toward Seventh Avenue.

"Get out here, Nikki. I don't want to stop in front of the house. Stay with Sheila. Don't leave her for a minute. And here, take the gun." Without taking his glance from Olga Otero, he slipped the gun to Nikki. "Just point it; don't try to shoot. The safety catch is on. I'll phone you to find out what the lady wanted of Sheila."

Nikki put the pistol into her purse and got to the curb.

"Follow the woman in black," Ellery said to the driver, and closed the door.

At Fourteenth Street, the Otero woman boarded an eastbound bus. At the southeast corner of Union Square, she got off. Ellery paid his cabdriver and followed the woman down the steps of the I. R. T. subway. On the platform, she let an express train pass and took a local.

As Ellery got into the car behind the one in which she was riding, he wondered why a person who could afford to stay at the Hollingsworth would travel about the city in buses and subways. Apparently Miss Otero was suddenly out of funds. Moreover, she had said that this was her first trip to New York and had asked Mr. Cobb to recommend a hotel. But obviously she was well acquainted with the transportation system. She had not stopped to ask directions.

When she got out at Canal Street and started to walk east, Ellery was convinced that she knew her way about the city very well. Now she was entering a part of it that was unfamiliar even to the majority of native New Yorkers.

Reaching Mott Street, she turned south. Chinese were scurrying here and there, standing in the doorways of the run-down buildings, talking rapidly in high sing-song voices with friends. The street was heavy with the smell of steam, fish, onions, aromatic foods, and spices. In the grocery windows were long, thin cabbages, soy beans, elongated yellow squashes, and boxes of litchi nuts. In the butcher stores smoked ducks hung from racks. Passing, Ellery got a whiff of raw meat. But mostly the smell of fish pervaded —clams that had popped open in the heat, live crabs, buckets of shrimps. . .

Miss Otero crossed Bayard Street and turned left onto Pell. Then suddenly she disappeared into a shop. The display window was filled with elaborately embroidered kimonos, carved ivory elephants and miniature shrines, an enormous assortment of rings of silver and semiprecious stones, carved teakwood trays, red cinnabar cigarette boxes, and a hundred odds and ends.

Ellery could see the woman standing at a counter. The Chinese behind it was examining something she had handed him. He looked up at her. She shook her head. He continued the examination. Then he held the object up to the light. Ellery saw that it was a jade necklace. As he went into the store, the Chinese was starting toward the back of the shop.

"Good afternoon, Miss Otero," Ellery said.

She started, and spun round.

"Oh!" she said in surprise. "You are the policeman detective who was with the inspector—how did he call himself? Ah, yes, Inspector Queen."

Ellery did not disillusion her.

"How much did he offer you for the necklace?" he asked, smiling.

"Three hundred," she said, returning the smile. "It is too little. I tell him four hundred. He say no, but goes to ask his partner."

"When he comes back, Miss Otero, tell him you've changed your mind about selling it. You're coming up to headquarters with me."

Her eyes narrowed.

"This is an impertinence. An imposition! I shall——"

"Never mind all that," Ellery said. "Come along quietly and you'll save yourself a lot of embarrassment. You have no idea how big a crowd can gather when they see the wagon drive up."

CHAPTER XII

AT HEADQUARTERS

As ELLERY and Miss Otero went into the waiting room on the second floor of Police Headquarters, the door of Inspector Queen's office opened, and Lois Ling, followed by three elderly Chinese and Sergeant Velie, came out.

The sergeant stopped dead in his tracks and stared, open-mouthed, at Olga Otero.

Ellery crossed to Lois Ling.

"Would you mind waiting a few minutes, Miss Ling? Possibly you can help the inspector to recover the stolen jewels."

Her eyes brightened.

"Of course, I'll wait. Oh, of course I want to help." She turned and spoke to her companions in Chinese.

They bowed ceremoniously to her and to Ellery and then left. Ellery seated Miss Ling and turned to the sergeant.

"Velie, please tell Dad that Miss Olga Otero and Mr. Queen are calling. And don't forget to close your mouth before you go into the inspector's office."

The sergeant's jaws snapped shut as he turned to leave. He was back almost immediately, holding the door open for Miss Otero and Ellery.

Inspector Queen got up as they came in. He motioned to chairs at either side of his big desk. The sergeant crossed the room and stood with his back to the window. He apparently could not take his eyes from Olga Otero.

"Dad," Ellery said as they sat down, "Miss Otero has brought a jade necklace to show you. You know, the one we were talking about."

The inspector blinked at Ellery and then turned toward the woman. She calmly opened her purse, took out the necklace, and handed it to him. He counted the twenty-six jade discs and examined the Chinese characters on the pendant.

"How did this come into your possession?"

"It was given to me by Mr. Cobb," she said wearily. "This man"—she nodded toward Ellery—"has put me to a great deal of inconvenience. I hope now that you are satisfied and that I may go."

"When did Mr. Cobb give you this?"

"On board the *Manchuria*. It was to be a souvenir of him."

"It has a great sentimental attachment for Miss Otero," Ellery explained gravely. "That's why she refused to sell it down in Chinatown—for less than four hundred dollars."

She turned to look venomously at Ellery.

"You are insulting," she said, and shrugged. "But what can I do?"

"You can tell the truth," Inspector Queen said.

"I am telling the truth."

"Is that so? Well, you say that Mr. Cobb gave you this aboard ship, yet it was in his possession when he landed."

Suddenly a look of fear came into her eyes.

"No," she insisted after a moment. "No, that is not so. He gave it to me the last day before we landed."

The inspector shook his head.

"We have proof that he did not. Positive proof. He declared it at the customs in San Francisco."

Miss Otero saw her opening and quickly took advantage of it.

"Yes, that is true. He wished to pay the duty himself. He took it through the customs for me."

Ellery swore inwardly. She had outwitted the inspector. The case against her had collapsed. When she had stolen the necklace, she had overlooked the fact that it would have been declared when it was brought into the country. There wasn't a chance, she had doubtless reasoned, of her being caught. Probably Cobb had told her it was to be a surprise gift for his daughter. So no one would know that he had it. But now, confronted with a customs declaration, she had cleverly used it to support her story. If she stuck to her story, there was absolutely no evidence against her.

"Dad," Ellery said, "I asked Miss Ling to wait outside. Do you mind if we have her in?"

The inspector looked sharply at Ellery. What was on his son's mind, he could not tell. Evidently Ellery had some plan, however. He turned to Velie.

"Ask Miss Ling to come here, Sergeant."

When Lois Ling had come from the waiting room, Ellery handed the necklace to her.

"Can you read the Chinese characters on the pendant?" he asked.

For several moments she studied them and

then said, "Yes. At first I couldn't make out what the second character meant. But I see now. It represents two sounds, *shee* and *lah*. 'Sheila,' of course. 'To *Sheila* from her loving father.' "

Olga Otero's white face turned whiter. But she quickly recovered.

"Of course, I did not know," she said, "that Mr. Cobb had planned to give the trinket to his daughter. Had I known that, I should not have accepted the gift."

"Naturally," said the inspector. "And now that you do know?"

"I shall be happy if you will restore it to Miss Cobb. I give it to her freely."

"It didn't occur to you to give it to her when you saw her a while ago, did it?" Ellery asked. "Why did you go to see her?"

"I went to express my sympathy," Miss Otero said. "Am I at liberty to go now?"

"Oh, quite," said the inspector. He turned to Velie. "Take Miss Otero's address, Sergeant, and have a receipt for the necklace mailed to her."

As soon as the door closed behind Olga Otero, Inspector Queen snatched up one of the telephones on his desk.

"Woman in black just leaving," he said. "Have two men tail her."

Ellery picked up a pad of paper from the desk and handed it with his fountain pen to Lois Ling.

"One more favor, Miss Ling. Please write the Chinese characters for Hotel Monkey."

Lois Ling laughed.

"Never heard of it."

"Neither did I," Ellery admitted. He took the pad on which she had written and looked at the characters. "Very odd language," he said, smiling, as he walked toward the door with her. "Thanks a lot."

"Hotel Monkey! Let's see that pad," Inspector Queen said when Lois Ling had gone.

Ellery handed it to him.

Velie craned over the inspector's shoulder.

"Well, can you beat that. How do you suppose they do it?"

"What did you want it for, El?" the inspector asked.

"I want you to have it put in the Chinese paper, under *personals* if they have such a thing—otherwise have it inserted as an ad with lots of white space around it."

"But what's the idea, son?"

"Just an experiment. If it works, swell. If it doesn't, I'll go back to my novel—which is crying 'papa!' "

"El gets a bit batty at times, Chief," Velie said. "It's best to humor him."

Ellery picked up a phone and called Sheila's apartment. Nikki answered.

"Hello, Nikki, this is Ellery."

"You mean personally—in the flesh?"

"Don't get canary. What did Miss Otero want?"

"Oh, she was sweet as pie and awfully sympathetic, Sheila says. She's very nice, she says, in a snaky sort of way."

"But what did she want?"

"Nothing. What would she want?"

"Let me speak to Sheila, Nikki."

"I thought that was coming!"

There was a pause. Then Sheila's voice.

"Hello, Mr. Queen."

"Sheila, what did Miss Otero want?"

"Nothing that I could find out. She told me how sorry she was, and talked about Dad and how nice he'd been to her on the boat."

"How many rooms have you?"

"Sitting room, bedroom, kitchenette, and bath. Why?"

"Did she go into any room besides the sitting room?"

After a short pause she said, "Why, yes. As a matter of fact she went into all the rooms. She wants to get an apartment herself. She said she liked mine. It was just the size she wanted. So, of course, I showed her around."

"Show her the closets?"

"Oh, naturally. You men don't understand how important they are."

"Hmm. Sheila, don't either you or Nikki leave the apartment until you hear from me, and don't let anyone in unless you recognize the voice before you open the door."

"All right, Mr. Queen. I am grateful——"

"Thanks, Sheila," he interrupted her. " 'Bye."

"Dad," Ellery asked the inspector, as he hung up the receiver, "how did Lois Ling's story check?"

"A hundred per cent. But I'm not overlooking any bets in this case."

A phone on the desk rang. Velie picked up the receiver.

"Inspector Queen's office. Oh, Piggott. What's on *your* mind? You don't say? Well, that's bad. Huh? Wait a minute." The sergeant clapped his enormous hand over the mouthpiece and looked at the inspector.

"It's Piggy phoning from Macy's. Brett went out. Piggy lost him in the crowd at Macy's. He's waiting for orders."

The inspector scowled.

"Tell him to go back to the Swiftfield and to phone in when Brett returns. Tell him—no, I'll tell him that personally when I see him."

Another phone rang. The inspector answered it.

"Hello, hello, Queen speaking. Oh, it's you, Hesse! He is, is he? Well, keep an eye on him, but stay where you are." He hung up and turned to Ellery. "Hesse's covering the lobby at the Hollingsworth. Sanders came in. He's sitting in the lobby reading a paper."

"Does he know who R. M. Smith is?" Ellery asked.

"He wouldn't be much of a newspaperman if he didn't."

"And of course he knows Brett by sight," Ellery said thoughtfully, "—and Olga Otero. And they both know that he knows them. Smith would guess. At least he wouldn't take a chance. So that leaves Ritter or someone working with Olga Otero."

"What are you mumbling about, El?" the inspector demanded.

"Ventro!" Ellery said explosively. "Chinese! Ventro!"

Velie said, "He's off his chump again."

"What about Ventro?" The inspector looked eagerly at his son.

"That's what the Chinese call Gordon Cobb. Say, Dad, I've got a date. See you at dinner." Ellery turned and hurried toward the door. "Don't forget the Chinese ad, Dad," he called back. "I've a hunch this case is going to break!"

CHAPTER XIII

THE MURDERER'S MARK

ELLERY's cab had made good time up Lafayette Street from police headquarters. Now, as it started up Fourth Avenue, the driver was able to cover ten blocks before the lights changed to red.

Ellery was impatient. No doubt it had been recalled by some, if not all the suspects in the case, that Cobb went under the name of Ventro in China. That was how the Chinese would think of him. Apparently Sanders had suddenly realized it, and Sanders knew that one of Cobb's bags had disappeared on the *Manchuria*. Moreover, Cobb had shown not the slightest concern over the disappearance and had lied to Sanders about having sent it to the hold. Now, suppose Cobb had turned the bag over to a Chinese. The Chinese confederate would unquestionably return it to Cobb, because it would contain something besides the jewels—something that had not been in the penthouse, but which Cobb would value very much for sentimental reasons if not for its intrin-

sic worth. In that case the Chinese, when returning the bag, would think in terms of Ventro, not
Gordon Cobb.

At Thirty-fourth Street the cab speeded up as
it entered Park Avenue. It roared north for six
blocks, then turned onto the Grand Central
viaduct. Ellery glanced up at the station clock.

Four-seventeen, standard; five-seventeen, day-
light.

The tires and brakes squealed as the cab rounded the sharp curves. The lights had just turned
green as the taxi came off the viaduct. The driver
made Fifty-fifth Street before he had to stop.

Ellery leaned forward.

"Go to the rear entrance of the hotel," he told
the driver.

A few minutes later, Ellery slipped past a
truck that was parked in the Hollingsworth's service entrance and went into the receiving room.
He hurried down a flight of iron stairs and then
along a corridor. At the end of it, he opened a
door and stepped into a white-tiled hall. To the
right was the barber shop. Farther along, he
passed the basement restaurant—*Bar-Grille,* the

sign read. He started up the marble steps to the left.

Was Sanders' interest in the case only that of a reporter, Ellery wondered. When several millions' worth of jewels were involved, it was just as well not to count too much on a man's professional integrity.

As Ellery's head came level with the floor of the lobby, he stopped and peered cautiously between two marble balusters. Across the room, two elderly ladies were seated on a couch. At the rear, a man, apparently a new arrival, was waiting for the elevator. Beside him a bellboy held a suitcase. Behind the office desk, Detective Hesse was trying to look like a hotel clerk. He would have looked less out of character, Ellery decided, in the guise of a bartender. In a chintz-covered chair, between the cigar stand, diagonally to the right, and the check room, sat Sanders, apparently absorbed in a copy of the *Saturday Evening Post*.

Ellery was trying to catch Hesse's eye, when the door of the elevator opened. A man got out. The new arrival and the bellboy got in. Ellery became tense. The man was Ritter.

Fanning himself with his straw hat, Ritter crossed the lobby toward Sanders. He took out a handkerchief and patted the bald spot on the back of his head. Sanders did not look up from the magazine as Ritter passed. Ritter stopped in front of the check room and spoke to the attendant. The attendant disappeared behind some racks. When he reappeared, he was carrying a cowhide bag. It answered the description Sanders had given of the bag that vanished from Cobb's stateroom.

A bellboy ran across the lobby to Ritter and reached for the bag. Ritter shook his head, put on his hat, and, picking the bag up, started for the Fifth Avenue entrance.

Sanders immediately lost all interest in the magazine. He tossed it onto the chair as he got up and hurried toward the entrance as soon as Ritter had gone through the revolving door.

In the office, Hesse immediately picked up the telephone receiver. Coming up into the lobby, Ellery signaled to him and hurried toward Fifth Avenue. Through the revolving door he saw Ritter get into a yellow cab. Sanders was not in sight. A moment later, when Ellery saw a second yellow cab come round the corner and head north on the Avenue, he glimpsed Sanders on the back seat. He stepped out onto the sidewalk and watched the two cabs proceed north for three blocks, where they stopped for a red light. Then he hailed a taxi and told the driver to follow, keeping at least two blocks between himself and the cars ahead. At Seventy-second Street, Sanders again showed his resourcefulness. When the traffic stopped, with a dozen or so cars between his cab and Ritter's to shield him, he got out of the yellow cab and jumped into a green one. Obviously, Sanders had no idea that he himself was being followed. The transfer was made in full view of the cars behind him. If it fooled Ritter, so much the better.

At Eighty-sixth Street, Ritter's cab turned east. At Lexington Avenue, while the traffic light was red, Sanders again made a transfer—this time to a crosstown bus. That maneuver, Ellery decided, was brilliant if it worked. But it was risky. There was too big a chance of the taxi's getting away in spite of the fact that the traffic was forced to stop at the end of each long crosstown block.

But luck favored Sanders, while Ellery's cab

followed leisurely behind the bus. At York Avenue, Ritter left his cab, bag in hand, and walked south. Sanders got out of the bus and followed in a cab. Several blocks south, Ritter turned toward the East River. It was obvious that he must soon reach his destination, as the river was only a block east. Apparently Sanders came to the same conclusion, for he got out of the cab and followed on foot as soon as Ritter had disappeared around the corner.

Ellery gave his driver instructions. The cab shot by Sanders, then a half a block farther, past Ritter, and turned north on East End Avenue.

Ellery got out and started to walk back. As he turned onto the cross street, he saw Ritter coming toward him on the opposite sidewalk. Sanders was not in sight. Ellery went up the steps of a brownstone house and stepped into the vestibule. Watching through the glass panel, he saw Ritter go up the steps of a house across the street. Except for the tenement building beside it, it was like all the other brownstone houses in the block. The whole neighborhood was little better than a slum. Paper littered the street. A small boy, bouncing a ball on the sidewalk, looked up at

Ritter. "Hello, Mr. Corri," he called. Ritter waved to the boy and went into the house.

Sanders came out from behind some steps halfway to York Avenue. He walked up to the boy and talked to him in a voice too low for Ellery to hear. After a few minutes, he followed Ritter into the house.

Ellery came out of the vestibule and sat down on the top step.

"Hey, son," he called to the boy.

The boy stopped bouncing the ball. Ellery beckoned to him. The boy started across the street, bouncing the ball as he came.

"What did your friend want, son?"

The boy turned his freckled face up at Ellery and scratched his red head.

"What friend?"

"The man you were talking with a moment ago."

"He ain't a friend. I never seen him before."

"Well, what did he want?"

"Whatcha want to know for?"

Ellery smiled.

"I'll give you a dime if you tell me."

"All right. My name's Charlie."

"Charlie, you're a pal. What did he ask you?"

"Where's the dime, mister?"

Ellery tossed one down to him. The boy caught it and put it in his pocket.

"He wanted to know who Mr. Corri was."

"Well, who is Mr. Corri?"

"He lives over in that house across the street."

"Is that all he asked you?"

"Naw. He asked what room he lived in. I told him the top floor at the back. You don't live here, do you, mister?"

"No. Do you like ice cream sodas?"

"Sure."

"There's a drugstore up on the corner of York. It has a soda fountain, hasn't it?"

"Sure."

"Well, here's another dime." Ellery flipped it, sending it spinning in a high arc. "Now, beat it up there and have one on me."

"Gee. Thanks, mister." He began to run toward York Avenue.

Ellery went into the vestibule and waited. In less than a minute, the door of the house across the street opened and Sanders came out. At the top of the steps he paused to look up and down

the street. Evidently he was nervous and undecid-
ed as to which way to go. Suddenly he made up
his mind, ran down the steps, and darted into the
areaway between the house and the tenement.

Ellery waited for a moment or two and then
crossed the street. The front door of the brownstone house was not locked. He went in. The
bare hall smelled musty. Cracked stairs led to the
upper floors. Although Ellery kept close to the
wall, and stepped carefully, the stair boards
creaked. When he reached the top floor, he saw
that the door of the room at the rear was ajar.
He stood still and listened. Nothing. He tiptoed
to the door and gently pushed it open. The room
was dark. Only a dim light came through the
deep green shade at the window. Somewhere a
clock was ticking. Otherwise there was silence.

Ellery hesitated. This could very well be a trap.
If he stepped through the doorway, he might be
bashed on the head. He'd have felt more comfortable if he'd brought a gun.

"Hey, Ritter," he called softly, "it's Brett."
No answer.

"Ritter!" He called more loudly this time.
Still no answer

Ellery stepped back and lit a match. He held it above his head, moving cautiously forward. The match spluttered and went out, but he had glimpsed a white patch in the darkness. It was round and appeared to be on the floor. He struck a second match and stepped into the room. The white patch was the bald spot at the back of Ritter's head. He was lying face down on the floor. Most of his body was out of sight behind a table that stood between it and Ellery.

Ellery went around the table and held the match close to Ritter's face. It was blue. Purple streaks at the throat showed that he had been strangled. Then suddenly Ellery's eyes widened. There was another mark on Ritter's neck. It was a scarlet hairline that extended from below the ear to the top of the collar.

Again the murderer had left his mark.

CHAPTER XIV

MARKED CARDS

FROM THE telephone booth in the corner drugstore Ellery Queen called his father.

"Hello there, son," the inspector said as soon as he recognized Ellery's voice. "Glad you called. You were right about a Chinese being in the crew of the *Manchuria*. He worked in the ship's laundry."

"That explains a lot, Dad. But listen. Remember Ritter, the cardsharp working for R. M. Smith?"

"Sure. What about him?"

"Someone strangled him a few minutes ago."

"Strangled him! Where are you? Where was he strangled?"

Ellery gave the inspector the address.

"I'll wait for you there, Dad. Fourth floor rear. And you'd better send out an alarm for Jim Sanders. Have him picked up and brought there."

"He in on this?"

149

"You might say so," murmured Ellery.

"I'm not surprised!"

While waiting for the inspector to arrive, Ellery made a thorough examination of Ritter's room and belongings. He had plenty of time to do so. It was a half hour before he heard the stairs creak. The inspector and Velie came in puffing. He told them how Sanders had followed Ritter from the Hollingsworth up to the room, and then had fled through the areaway.

"But Ritter's not just Ritter," he said in conclusion. "He's Corri, the magician. Ever hear of the 'Ingenious Corri?' "

"Sure—years ago—vaudeville. *I* told you that Ritter was Corri." The inspector got down on his knees beside the body.

"I know," Ellery said. "I'm underlining it, because it's important. There's a drawerful of newspaper clippings, advance notices, and so on, over there." He pointed to a fumed-oak dresser that, lacking one caster, leaned at an angle against the stained wallpaper.

"Was the light on and the window shade drawn when you got here, El?"

"The shade was drawn, but the light was out.

It's mighty interesting about that light bulb, though."

"What is? Say, El, look here."

"What, Dad?"

The inspector pointed to Ritter's neck.

"That scratch! It's like the one on Cobb's neck."

"Yes, and on Sheila Cobb's wrist. Curious, isn't it?"

"He was choked all right," Velie said, looking down at the body, "but I don't savvy the scratch."

The inspector got up.

"What were you going to say about the light, Ellery?"

"The switch is over there by the door." Ellery pointed to it. "You can reach in from the hall and turn it on without coming into the room."

"So what?" Velie growled.

"When I turned the switch after finding Ritter's body, the light didn't go on. That's so what."

The sergeant looked up at the fixture. It was in the middle of the room, hanging from about three feet of wire. A green-glass shade reflected the light onto the table below. A layer of dust covered the table and the three magazines on it.

"What you're telling us, I suppose, is that someone'd unscrewed the bulb," the inspector said.

"Right," said Ellery Queen. "And that fact is
significant if you consider it in relation to other
facts."

"Such as?" Velie asked hastily.

"Such as the fact that Ritter hasn't been staying
here for several days. Everything's covered with
grit and dust—the dresser, the table, that wooden
chair over there, and the window sill. Next, we
can be pretty sure that he didn't unscrew the bulb
himself. Someone else did. It hadn't just worked
itself away from contact, as they sometimes do. I
twisted it about four times to screw it back into
the socket. You see, it's so high up I had to stand
on tiptoe and lean over the table."

"Sure," said Velie, "spoiling any fingerprints
that might be on the bulb. Master-mind!"

"There wouldn't be any," Ellery said calmly.
"The murderer didn't touch a thing in the place.
He knew his business. The bulb had been wiped
clean. He probably had a handkerchief in his
hand when he unscrewed it."

"So you think Sanders came here and fixed it

so that it would be dark. Well, how did he get in?"

"Whoever unscrewed the light came in from the fire escape."

The inspector crossed to the window and put up the shade. Outside, an iron fire escape descended to the yard behind the house. He examined the window sill.

"Looks like you're right, El." The inspector pointed to a streak in the dust. "He took pains not to touch or step on the sill. But his trouser cuff, maybe, made that streak when he swung his leg over. Sanders must have unscrewed the bulb and then drawn the shade when he left to make sure the place would be dark."

"I'd say the murderer unscrewed the bulb, all right, but I think he found the shade drawn."

"How do you figure that, son?"

"He'd realize that Ritter would know instantly when he opened the door that something was wrong if Ritter hadn't drawn the shade himself. It would have put him on his guard. The unscrewed bulb wouldn't. Ritter would merely figure that it had burned out. Besides, it's probable Ritter kept the shade drawn most of the time. He's a gambler. You can figure that he's up most of the night and sleeps in the daytime. He'd put the shade down to keep the light out. Then when he left, he might reasonably leave it down to keep the hot sun out. The window faces south, and this is the top floor. It must get pretty hot, right under the roof."

Velie said grudgingly, "Maybe so. But I don't see that it matters. The point is it's pretty clear how Sanders got the bag out of here without your seeing him lug it off."

"Is it?" Ellery asked. "You think he heaved it out the window and then ran through the areaway to the backyard, picked it up, and made off. It's certainly possible."

"El, what about the bag? You say it answered the description of the one that disappeared from Cobb's stateroom on the boat. But how do you figure Ritter knew it was in the check room at the Hollingsworth? Naturally, we asked there, and nothing had been checked either by or for Gordon Cobb."

"It wouldn't be, Dad. That's where the Chinese gentleman comes in. The Chinese call Gordon

Cobb 'Ventro.' Now, if a Chinese, coming to this country from China, had borrowed something from Ventro, and knew that he had engaged the penthouse at the Hollingsworth, what would he do? He wants to return the bag and its contents secretly to Cobb. He goes to the check room and leaves the bag for Mr. Ventro, as they have previously arranged. He doesn't know that Cobb is dead, so he thinks everything is all right. Anyhow, that's what happened. After I phoned you, I called Hesse at the Hollingsworth. He talked to the check room man and confirmed it. If I could figure it out, so could the murderer. He seems a lot smarter than any of us. Ritter figured it out— so why not the other suspects? Or maybe Ritter's working with Olga Otero."

"Say," Velie said brightening, "that Otero broad—she gave our boys the slip, but she's registered at the hotel she said she'd moved to. You know, if we didn't have the goods on Sanders— those scratches! A woman's sharp fingernails!"

"Sure," Ellery said ironically, "you've got something there. Dad, did Brett show up at the Swiftfield after he pulled his act at Macy's?"

The inspector scowled.

"He hadn't up to the time I left headquarters," he said and turned to the sergeant. "Velie, go down and boot the janitor up here. Then call Centre Street. Have the morgue wagon sent."

"Another little job for Doc Prouty," Velie said, grinning, as he went into the hall. "You're gonna catch it for sure, Inspector!"

Ellery Queen went to the dresser and, opening the top drawer, took out a pack of cards.

Handing them to the inspector, he said, "Dad, there's one thing that a magician and a cardsharp have in common, and that's nimble fingers. Smith is a cardsharp. Ritter—or Corri—was both. That's why in sleight of hand he would have it over Smith. But working together in a poker game they'd be hot stuff. Take a look at these cards."

Inspector Queen examined them carefully.

"They're marked," he announced and continued to study them. "Pretty neat. One pin prick on the backs of the aces, two on the kings."

"Yes, the system's simple enough, but the interesting point is that undoubtedly both Ritter and Smith could deal any hand they wanted to. Teaming together, they wouldn't need marked cards. So it seems they didn't always work together. They probably had friendly games with their own bunch. They'd all be on to Ritter's and Smith's crooked deals, so neither would try that. But one of them managed to put it over on the others by using marked cards."

"What of it, El?" the inspector asked, putting the cards into his pocket. "We know they're crooks without this evidence."

"I think the marked cards are important," Ellery insisted. "When sharpers sit around a table, they're not apt to overstrain their confidence in one another. They break open a new pack of cards. So the one who marked the cards had to do it after the playing had started."

The inspector smiled.

"I don't think even the Ingenious Corri could palm a pin, son."

"No, he couldn't," Ellery agreed emphatically. "That's why the marks are so important!"

CHAPTER XV

ELLERY and Inspector Queen turned as the door opened and Sergeant Velie pushed a colored man in blue overalls and a brown shirt into the room.

"Here's the janitor," Velie announced. "His name's Dobb."

Apparently Velie had not forewarned Dobb that Ritter had been murdered. Velie's push sent him several steps into the room before he could stop himself. Then, gaping at the body, he recoiled in terror until he collided with the sergeant's great bulk. For a moment he stood speechless, opening and closing his mouth without uttering a sound.

"Dobb," the inspector said sharply, "can you identify this body?"

The man nodded.

"Who is he?"

The Negro's lips made little puffing sounds before he could articulate.

"Lawd of mercy, is he daid?"

"Murdered," said the inspector.

At the word, Dobb's whole body jerked.

"Who is he?" the inspector demanded.

"Mr. Corri, boss. That man's Mr. Corri."

"When did you last see him?"

"I ain't seen him. Not for a week."

"Do you take care of the rooms?"

"No, sir. I's the super. I sweep out the halls and collect the garbage. I don't go into the rooms."

"When were you last in here?"

"I ain't been in here. I don't go into the rooms, boss. I ain't been in here since Mr. Corri rented this room. The gents take care of their own."

"What do you know about Corri's habits?"

"Nothin', boss. I don't know nothin'."

"Where were you this afternoon?"

"In the houses across the street. I got six buildings to take care of."

Much to Dobb's relief, the sound of someone running up the stairs interrupted the questioning.

A husky patrolman stood in the doorway.

"We've got your man outside in the car, Inspector Queen," he said. "Shall I bring him up?"

"Yes." The inspector turned back to Dobb as the officer left. "Where do you live?"

"I got a room in the basement, boss."

"Did Corri have many visitors?"

"I don't know, sir."

"Did you ever see any?"

"I saw a big man come here once."

"Do you know his name?"

"No, sir."

"Can you describe him?"

"He was a mighty big man, boss."

"Big nose?" Ellery suggested.

"Yes, sir. Mighty big nose."

"When was he here?" the inspector asked.

" 'Bout a month ago, boss."

Once more Inspector Queen turned toward the door as Jim Sanders, followed by the patrolman, came into the room.

Sanders glanced at the body and then, without speaking, looked at the inspector.

"Ever seen this man before, Dobb?" the inspector demanded, pointing to Sanders.

"No, sir. That's not him."

"All right, Dobb, go about your business. I'll want to see you later." He turned to the sergeant, "Velie, go along with him. Take a look around his room for the missing bag." When the door closed, he said, "What do you know about this, Sanders?" and pointed to the body.

Sanders frowned.

"Not a thing. Why should I?"

"Ever see him before?"

"Nope."

"That's a lie."

Sanders closed his eyes.

Inspector Queen turned to the patrolman.

"Where'd you pick him up?"

"We were waiting for him in his room, sir. When he walked in, we grabbed him."

"Did he have a suitcase or bag?"

"No, sir."

"Where'd you park the bag, Sanders?" the inspector asked softly. Sanders opened his eyes.

"What bag? What's this all about, Inspector?"

"Keep it up," the inspector said, "and you'll talk yourself right into the hot seat. You're all innocence, aren't you? Well, we know that you followed this man from the Hollingsworth. You strangled him, threw the bag he had out the window, and then went around behind the house and got it. So cut the baby-face act. Where did you leave the bag?"

Sanders went white. He stared frantically about. "The bag! Gosh! Is it gone? Wasn't it here?"

"Where'd you leave it?" The inspector advanced toward Sanders.

Sanders' strength suddenly left him. He flopped onto the bed. Then quickly he got down on his knees and looked under the bed. Sitting on the bed once more, he looked at the inspector with a naked terror.

"Listen, Inspector Queen," he said, his voice thick, "I didn't do it. I swear I didn't."

"Sanders," the inspector said, "you've tossed enough bull my way already. You say you followed Gordon Cobb all the way from China just for a story your paper could have covered just as well here. Out of curiosity you got a job bellhopping at Cobb's hotel. Not so that you'd have access to his rooms; certainly not. Then Cobb's murdered, and you get all full of curiosity about that. You follow Ritter here and come up to this room at the exact time he's murdered, and you tell me you've never even seen the man."

Sanders was shaking.

"Let me tell you, Inspector Queen," he pleaded. "I lied about not having seen him. Corri, I thought his name was. I was too scared to tell the truth. Everything else was true. I swear it. I'll tell you all I know about this. You must believe me."

"All right, start out by telling me where you hid the suitcase."

"Listen, Inspector, I never saw this man before today. I was dead certain Olga Otero was acting as a spy for the Japanese. They'd have to have a non-Japanese for the job. A Jap would be too conspicuous. Well, when the police began to question her, the Japs knew that, as far as they were concerned, she was finished. Naturally if she was under suspicion, they'd have to work with someone else."

"Look here, Sanders," the inspector interposed, "no use starting another cock-and-bull story."

"Let him tell his story, Dad," Ellery said. "It makes sense—to me."

Sanders looked at him gratefully.

"What I figured," he said, "was that they'd have someone covering the Otero woman in case she tried a double-cross. In that case, the man keeping an eye on her would have been on the *Manchuria*. Believe me, I studied the faces of every passenger aboard. I'd know any one of them.

"Next, I figured Cobb had arranged with the purser, or someone else the spies wouldn't suspect, to clear the stuff through customs and then express it to him at the Hollingsworth. That's how I accounted for the disappearance of the bag from his cabin. He was worried about it, you see.

"Now, spies aren't anybody's fools. They could figure that out as well as I could. So the Japs would tell the Otero woman to lay off, and have the spy who was covering her carry on her job. Well, that person would be sure to show up at the Hollingsworth, and I went there to spot him. I was sitting in the lobby, with both eyes and ears open, when I hear the guy Corri, or Ritter as you call him, ask for a bag left for Mr. Ventro. I'd never seen this bird before in my life, but I nearly jumped out of my skin when I heard him say 'Ventro.' I followed him here. But it beats me how you found out. I asked a kid out in front who the man was. He said his name was Corri and that he lived on the fourth floor, back. I came up. The door was open part way. What I'd planned was to pretend to be an insurance salesman. I just wanted to get a look around and see what the layout was. Then I was going to phone you and stand guard outside until the police arrived. The room was dark. That struck me as cock-eyed. I called, 'Mr. Corri.' I called again. Then I came in and lit a match. I nearly dropped dead. He was lying on the floor just as he is now. I was in a panic. I knew what you'd think—just what you are thinking. I got out as fast as I could."

"Why did you go around into the court?" the inspector asked.

"People were coming from York Avenue and others from East End. I wanted to get away without anyone's getting close enough to get a good look at me. I ducked into the areaway and came out on the next street."

"Sure, picking up the bag on the way," said the inspector. "Sanders, you're a first-class liar, but you're not going to get away with it." The inspector turned to the officer. "Take him down to headquarters," he ordered. "Keep at him until he tells where he put the suitcase."

"Dad," Ellery asked, "what's the charge you're going to make against Sanders?"

"Homicide," the inspector announced positively. "I'm charging him with the murder of Gordon Cobb and of Corri, alias Ritter."

Sanders jumped to his feet.

"Mr. Queen," he begged, clutching Ellery's arm, "you've got to help me. I'm innocent. You've got to prove I am. I'm broke. I can't even hire a lawyer. If you don't save me, they'll send me to the chair. Find that bag, Mr. Queen. Find it and you'll find the murderer."

Ellery saw that Sanders' nerve was on the verge of breaking. His eyes were horror-stricken.

"Keep your chin up, Sanders," he said. "Dad, if I were you I'd change the charge to suspicion of homicide."

Inspector Queen considered the point.

"I don't see that it makes much difference, El," he said after a moment.

"All right, then," Ellery said, "make it suspicion of homicide."

"Very well," the inspector agreed. "Take him along," he said to the officer.

"Help me, please, Mr. Queen," Sanders said hoarsely as the patrolman caught his arm and dragged him from the room. "I'm innocent!"

The inspector frowned at Ellery.

"Why did you want me to change the charge against him?"

"Holding Sanders is all to the good," Ellery said. "It'll put the real murderer of Ritter off guard. Dad, I'm going to see Walsh at his office in the morning and have a talk with him. I'll make an appointment for nine-thirty. At nine-forty I wish you'd call him on the phone. Tell him you've arrested Sanders and ask him to come to headquarters immediately."

"Now what are you up to, son?" the inspector asked skeptically.

"Dad, Sanders didn't kill Ritter, and I've a hunch who did. But the one vital bit of evidence is missing. I can't fix the killing on the murderer without it."

Inspector Queen puckered his forehead in irritation.

"But Sanders——"

"Listen, Dad," Ellery interrupted. "Forget Sanders. He didn't do it. Three things point infallibly to his innocence—the drawn window shade, the dust on the chair and the table, and the electric bulb."

CHAPTER XVI

WALSH PULLS A BONER

AT EXACTLY nine-thirty the following morning, Mr. Ellery Queen got out of the elevator on the twenty-third floor of the Jackson Building on West Forty-second Street. On the frosted-glass panel of room 2324, HENRY WALSH in black letters announced the agent's place of business. Turning the knob, Ellery found that the door was locked. He knocked.

Inside, Walsh pressed a button on his desk. A series of metallic clicks came from the latch. Ellery opened the door and walked in.

"Good morning, Mr. Walsh." Ellery turned to close the door. As he did so, he surreptitiously pressed the button that held the latch. "Another hot day. Looks as though we were in for a spell."

"Hot spell's right." Walsh got up from behind the desk, mopping the back of his neck. "It gets me down. I sweat like a horse." He extended a moist, flabby hand to Ellery. "Have a seat, Mr.

168

Queen." He motioned to a chair beside the mahogany desk and sat down again. "Glad to see you. What can I do for you? It's about poor old Cobb, I suppose."

"Perhaps there's a connection. I don't know," Ellery said as he sat down.

Walsh opened a box of cigars.

"Smoke?" he asked, holding it toward Ellery.

"No, thanks. I stick to a pipe and cigarettes." He took a package of cigarettes from his pocket.

Walsh bit off the end of his cigar.

"Well, you can count on me to do everything in my power to help get the murderer of Gordon Cobb. They don't come any finer than Gordon. I was just talking with his daughter, Sheila, on the phone. Fine girl, Sheila is. Fine girl. What's on your mind, Mr. Queen?"

"You used to be a booker for vaudeville artists."

"That's right. Those were the days! Gone with the wind." Walsh sighed. "Cobb was my last client. Now I handle opera stars and musicians—concert artists, that is. Temperamental bunch."

Ellery smiled.

"From magicians to musicians, you might say."

"How's that?"

"You used to have magicians in vaudeville, didn't you?"

Walsh laughed.

"Sure, sure. Magicians, tap dancers, acrobats, song-and-dance teams, and so on. That's good—magicians to musicians!"

"Ever know a man named Corri?"

"Corri? Corri? Can't say I remember him."

"Is that so?" Ellery looked surprised. "I understand he was quite famous in his day. Corri the Ingenious, or the Ingenious Corri, or something."

Walsh wrinkled his forehead while he searched his memory.

"Sounds familiar. He was a magician, you say?"

Ellery nodded.

"Sleight of hand artist."

"There was a Corrigan on the Poli circuit."

"Nope, Corri," Ellery said. "This man went by the name of Corri. Have you still got your old records, Mr. Walsh?"

"Sure, sure. I'd have a card on him if he ever amounted to anything. Just a minute." Walsh got up and went to a filing cabinet. "Sometimes the movies want to get hold of an old-timer. My files come in handy." He flipped forward the cards under *C*. "Sure enough. You're right. Here we are. Corri. He was a magician. Fifteen-minute act." He shut the file and returned to his desk. "He must have listed his act with my secretary. She was a tough one to get by. Some of the boys in the old days wanted to put on their whole act for you. Well, the card's there, all right; but I never booked him. Why, what did you want to know about him?"

"I wanted to find out what he's been doing since he quit vaudeville."

Walsh was thoughtful for a moment.

"Well, I can make inquiries through some of the boys that used to be in the same game. He'd have friends, of course, and I might locate one who knows what's become of him."

"I wish you would, Mr. Walsh. It's important."

"Sure, sure. I'll get a line on him for you—if he's still alive. But if you're thinking that he might have known Cobb, it's not likely. Cobb never played in this country, and it's not likely he knew the bunch here. He sort of steered shy of the crowd."

Ellery watched Walsh's face closely.

"You say if he's still alive—well, that's just the point. He isn't."

Walsh looked up quickly.

"I don't understand. Not alive? How do you mean, that's the point?"

"Ritter was murdered yesterday afternoon."

Walsh's blotched face became pale.

"Murdered? Ritter was murdered?" he said. He wiped his lips with his handkerchief and then patted his forehead.

"Yes. I thought there might be some connection between his and Cobb's murder."

Walsh blinked.

"But I don't see what Corri's death has to do with Cobb. He never—Excuse me." As the telephone rang, he turned and took off the receiver. "Oh, good morning, Inspector Queen. You don't say! You don't say! Well, that's fast work, Inspector. Congratulations. Yes, your son's here now. I'll tell him. Sure, sure. Sure I can. I'll come right down." He hung up.

"Was that Dad?" Ellery asked. "What did he want?"

"They've got Cobb's murderer. Someone

named Sanders. He wants me to come right down to headquarters." Walsh got up excitedly and snatched his hat from the clothes tree. "Will you come along, too?" he asked, opening the door.

"I've got a date uptown. I'll walk to the corner with you." Ellery saw with satisfaction that Walsh did not stop to examine the latch as he closed the door.

At the Times Square subway entrance, Ellery Queen left Walsh and immediately returned to the Jackson Building. Opening the door of Walsh's office, he released the catch, crossed to the filing cabinet, and took out Corri's card.

A glance told him that Walsh had booked Corri over a period of years. However, Ellery didn't require the evidence of the card to know that Walsh had been lying when he denied knowing the magician. When Ellery had suddenly announced that Corri had been murdered, he had used the name Ritter. And Walsh, taken aback, had also spoken of Ritter, instead of Corri. Then, in his excitement, caused by the inspector's call, he had apparently not realized his blunder.

Ellery put back the card and, going to the desk,

sat down in Walsh's swivel chair. The bottom drawer of the desk was locked, but in his haste Walsh had neglected to lock the drawer directly above it. Ellery removed the upper drawer, reached into the lower, and took out a letter file. Under *C* he found Walsh's correspondence with Gordon Cobb. Ellery quickly skipped through until he came to the last letter postmarked China. It gave a detailed list of Cobb's earnings for the past six months. Ten per cent of the total was written below the addition. Then came the sentence, "I'll give you a check to cover as soon as I arrive in New York." At the bottom of the page, Cobb began a new paragraph, only a part of the sentence appearing on the page: "Now here's something I'll ask you to keep absolutely under your——" The second sheet of the letter was missing. No doubt Walsh had destroyed it. Walsh would want to keep the first page because it was an acknowledgment of Cobb's indebtedness to him. He would probably burn the second, if it told about Cobb's bringing the jewels to America. Walsh wasn't supposed to know anything about the jewels. But it was a pretty sure thing that he had, Ellery reasoned, judging from the last line. The first word on the following page would obviously be "hat." So Cobb had confided in Walsh.

Ellery put the letter into his pocket, made sure that everything else was exactly as he had found it, and quickly closed the door behind him.

A few hours later, after a conference with Inspector Queen at police headquarters, Ellery rang the bell of Sheila Cobb's apartment on Fourth Street. Nikki opened the door.

"It's about time you showed up," she said, frowning at him. "Where have you been? What have you been doing? Why didn't you phone?"

Ellery sat down wearily in a chintz-covered chair, extended his long legs, and looked about the room. The chintz draperies, the bright lamp shades, and multi-colored hooked rugs gave the room a feminine atmosphere that was quite suitable for the very feminine Sheila.

Sheila did not conceal her distress when Ellery told the girls about Jim Sanders' arrest. Apparently, he decided, Sanders' sudden devotion was in some measure appreciated.

"Ladies," Ellery announced, "you won't have

to wait until much after three o'clock this afternoon for the case to break."

Nikki sat up.

"Three! It's two now! Why three o'clock?"

"I've induced Dad to assemble all the suspects
at the penthouse at that time—all except Olga
Otero. She won't be there."

"You mean she's eliminated as a suspect?"

"That depends upon what you suspect her of,"
Ellery said cryptically. "I certainly haven't eliminated her from the case, if that's what you have
in mind. Walsh will be there, Jim Sanders, a
gambler named R. M. Smith, Brett—he's being
held temporarily on a gambling charge—the
manager of the Hollingsworth, Lois Ling, and
an unidentified Chinese. I dropped in to take you
two up to the hotel if you want to come. I want
to get there before the others."

Nikki jumped up.

"Sheila," she said excitedly, "get your hat!"

"Just a minute," Ellery said, and turned to
Sheila. "I want to warn you about Mr. Walsh.
I wouldn't trust him, if I were you. But be perfect-
ly natural when you meet him this afternoon.
That's important. You see, Dad checked up with

the telegraph company this noon, after I'd had a talk with Walsh. They delivered a telegram to him from your father on the day he landed in San Francisco. It read, *Arriving August twelfth instead of fourteenth. Advise Sheila.*"

Sheila gasped. And then she burst into tears.

CHAPTER XVII

WAR OF NERVES

AT TWO-THIRTY, Inspector Queen, Ellery, Nikki, Sheila, and Sergeant Velie were in the living room of the penthouse that Gordon Cobb had so briefly occupied.

The inspector was nervously pacing about, blowing through his mustache, while Nikki and Sheila sat on the sofa, tense with excitement.

"I don't like this way of doing things, El," the inspector was complaining. "It's too theatrical."

"It's the modern technique, called the war of nerves," Ellery said. "Some of the suspects haven't been telling the truth. By getting them all together here, I'm planning to wear down their nerves until they snap. Then they'll all start talking to save their skins. As far as I'm concerned, there's only one piece of evidence lacking—and I hope to have that before long. I'm expecting to get enough corroborating testimony to insure the conviction of Mr. Cobb's murderer—even without a confession."

178

"That's all fine, El, if it works out. But if it doesn't, it's a mess," the inspector said, scowling.

"What beats me," said Velie, "is why all the fuss when we've got the goods on Sanders. Any jury would convict him."

"I don't know about that," Ellery grinned. "All the evidence against him is circumstantial. I'm expecting to produce some that isn't."

There was a knock at the door.

"Come in," Inspector Queen called.

Escorted by two plain-clothes men, Jim Sanders came into the room. He was looking pale and haggard, but somehow had managed to keep his clothes neat. He was wearing a fresh shirt and had recently shaved. His dark eyes searched Ellery's for some hope. Then he saw Sheila sitting with Nikki on the couch. As soon as the detective to whom he was handcuffed released him, he went to her.

"Sheila, you don't believe I killed your father!"

She tried to show her confidence in him by smiling at him. But the attempt was unsuccessful. She motioned for him to sit beside her.

Inspector Queen stationed one of the detectives in Cobb's bedroom, the other outside the hall door. Then a third detective came in with Brett. The inspector stationed the officer in the other bedroom and told Brett to sit down. Brett was nervous.

"What do you want me for, Inspector?" he asked. "I thought the charge was gambling——"

"Shut up, Brett, and sit down."

Harry Walsh was the next to arrive. Mopping his face, he strode up to Ellery and then looked about the room. He smiled and bowed to Sheila and Nikki.

"Sanders here yet?" he whispered to Ellery.

Ellery nodded.

"Good Lord! You're letting Miss Cobb sit beside the murderer?"

"She doesn't know he is," Ellery said.

Lois Ling came with her elderly father. They at once retired to chairs that Ellery placed for them in a corner of the room. With inscrutable faces, they watched the others.

R. M. Smith, dynamic and self-confident, came through the doorway. He swept the room with a glance and strode over to the inspector.

"Never had the pleasure of meeting you, Inspector Queen," he said. "Seen your pictures in the paper. Recognized you at once. Your men tell me you want to see me about some charge against Brett." He smiled. "Has the old fool been operating here at the Hollingsworth? I'll break his neck for him."

Smith towered over the inspector. Ellery noticed that he was almost as tall as Velie—about six-two at least. Ellery walked over to him and introduced himself.

"Glad to know you, Mr. Queen," Smith said heartily, putting out his hand. "I've read your books. How do you writers ever think up your ideas? You must lie awake nights."

Ellery squeezed Mr. Smith's hand.

"Sometimes I take them from life," he said, and, turning, saw that Parkman, the hotel manager, had just come into the room.

Parkman looked stiff and uncomfortable in his morning coat. The inspector motioned to a chair. The manager carefully pulled the tails of his coat aside before he sat down. Then, with ill-concealed distaste, he began to inspect the people assembled in the room.

Ellery took Sergeant Velie into the hall and handed him an envelope.

"Velie," he said, "in that envelope is a search warrant. I know how squeamish you and Dad are, so I got the warrant. You needn't be nervous. Downstairs in the lobby a couple of your pals are waiting for you. I want you to take them to the address on the warrant and search the place."

"Search it, El? What are we to search it for?"

"A cowhide suitcase, two by three by four. Open it. If the thing I think you'll find is there, we'll have the last piece of evidence we need against the murderer. In that case, have one of the boys call me immediately on the phone, and you bring it here without losing a moment's time. Now, go like blazes. I'll expect to hear from you in less than twenty minutes."

"But what's supposed to be in the bag, the jewels?"

"No. The thing that's been missing all along from Cobb's effects."

"But if I don't know what's missing, how will I know if the thing's the thing you think it is? How can I tell——"

"Never mind," Ellery soothed him. "You'll know, Sergeant." Velie brightened at this display of confidence, and made for the elevator.

Before opening the door, Ellery looked at the palm of his hand. Suddenly the muscles of his jaw hardened. He reached for the doorknob and turned it.

Standing with his back to the door, Ellery searchingly examined the faces of those seated about the room. And suddenly the room was filled with an invisible tension.

"To one of you," Ellery Queen began abruptly, "it is not news that the murderer of Gordon Cobb is among us." He paused while the others glanced uneasily at one another.

Jim Sanders leaned forward, gazing earnestly at Ellery.

"The murderer had advance information that Mr. Cobb would occupy this apartment. Those of you who indisputably had such knowledge are Sheila Cobb, Mr. Sanders, Mr. Brett, Mr. Parkman, Mr. Walsh, and Miss Otero, who is not present."

Walsh half rose from his chair.

"I deny that," he said quickly. "I didn't expect him until two days after he arrived, and I didn't know he was coming to the Hollingsworth until Miss Cobb phoned me."

"I see," said Ellery.

"Naturally, I knew that the reservation was made for Mr. Cobb and his daughter," Parkman said, adding indignantly, "why include me?"

"Since you knew, why should I not include you?" Ellery continued without waiting for an answer. "The murderer entered the apartment by breaking a pane of glass in the French window of Mr. Cobb's bedroom. Cobb, naturally, was not in the room at the time. The murderer either had sufficient time to replace the glass while Cobb was out, or he did so after committing the crime. Any of you could have done that, as a door in the hall gives access to the roof and the terraces. Those of you who were in a particularly favorable position to do so were Mr. Parkman, Mr. Sanders, masquerading as a bellboy, and Mr. Brett—Count Brett at the time, who had the other penthouse."

Brett squirmed in his chair. He opened his mouth to say something.

"Why, Brett, did you follow Gordon Cobb from China?" asked Mr. Queen. "Why, as a bogus count, did you take a penthouse at the Hollingsworth? Why did you run away immediately it became known he'd been murdered? And why did you hide under an assumed name at the Swiftfield?"

The questions came as a series of shocks.

"I didn't follow him home! You can't say I was following him just because I was on the same boat."

"Quite right," Ellery agreed amiably. "However, you went to China at considerable expense, flying most of the way. You had no discernible business in China, and to get a passport for China at this time is, to say the least, difficult. You stayed there only a short time, and somehow managed to get passage on the *Manchuria* on short notice. Presumably the only way you could do that was by paying someone a big bonus for his ticket. We must conclude, in consequence, that it was important for you to return on that boat. Your journey was obviously not a pleasure trip."

Brett's nervousness was increasing.

"Of course it wasn't. I had business in China."

"You might with justice be called a professional man, Mr. Brett," Ellery said with considerable sarcasm in his tone, "but hardly a business man. What was your business?"

"My business was confidential," Brett said, staring down at the rose-taupe rug.

"I quite agree," Ellery said. "Highly confidential; and incidentally, I know what it was. And now, what was your business here at the hotel? Of course, you didn't follow Gordon Cobb from San Francisco to New York, you just happened to come along with him and just happened to be bunking in an apartment next door to him at the time he was murdered."

Sweat broke out on Brett's forehead. The evidence was piling up against him. Think fast. Squirm out before the trap snapped shut!

"Well," he said shamefacedly, "I guess you know anyhow, Mr. Queen. I may as well come clean. I'm a gambler. Poker's my line. I met Cobb on the boat. I could see he was good pickings. He'd just got into the money. Easy come; easy go. I came here to cultivate him—coax him into a little game." He smiled and spread his hands.

"And the stakes in the little game you were playing—were they a collection of immensely valuable jewels?—valuable enough to tempt you to murder for them?"

Brett was stunned—speechless.

Ellery turned quickly to R. M. Smith. He had for the moment sufficiently frayed Brett's nerves. He could snap them now anytime.

"Brett is your partner, isn't he, Mr. Smith?"

"Partner? Well, hardly my partner," Smith said cautiously. "He's a friend, and I've known him for a good many years. He may put over a sharp one now and then—who doesn't? But murder—never. Not him. He's got too much sense, and not enough guts. You can bank on that. No, Mr. Queen, I'll vouch for Brett. You're barking up the wrong tree. Take it from me."

"For the benefit of anyone here who doesn't know it," Ellery said, addressing the room, "let me tell you that a second murder has been committed. The motive was the same. Possibly the murderer was, too." He turned to Sanders. "As I indicated, Mr. Sanders, you may or may not have committed the first murder. But about the second murder—that of Ritter, alias Corri——" He turned back to Smith. "Ritter was a friend of yours, wasn't he, Mr. Smith?"

Smith frowned.

"I knew him."

"Well," Ellery said, looking at Sanders, "I'm confident that you didn't kill Ritter, at any rate. I've several reasons for knowing that you didn't, besides the one I'm going to mention. Ritter's murderer knew who he was and where he lived. He also knew or suspected that Ritter had something of great value in his possession. Knowing that Ritter would take it to his room, he went there first, unscrewed the electric bulb so that the room, with the window shade drawn, would remain dark after Ritter turned the switch.

"Now, Mr. Sanders, among other things, it's what you didn't know that proves your innocence of that crime. You didn't know where he was going, or you wouldn't have gone to such pains to conceal the fact that you were following him. You would have gone to his room directly and waited for him. That is what the

murderer did, entering by the fire escape.
You didn't know who Ritter was or in
which room he lived, because you had to ask
a boy on the street in front of the house. You
entered the house about three minutes after Ritter went in. I'd say it took you about that long or
longer to come down the street from the steps
where you'd been hiding and to talk to the boy.

"Now, Inspector," he said, smiling at his
father, "I ask you in all fairness, what would you,
Ritter, or anyone else do who went into that room
and found that the lights didn't work? Wouldn't
you or he go immediately to the window and put
up the shade so as to let in some light? It's prepos-
terous to think that he would stand there in the
dark for three or four minutes."

"The point's well taken," the inspector said,
and blew through his mustache. "But it's possible that Sanders pulled down the shade after
strangling him and unscrewed the bulb, too, hoping to delay the discovery of the crime."

"The bulb proves that it's impossible, Inspector
Queen," Ellery said. "I'll return to that later. But,
in the meantime, the fact that the door was left

ajar somewhat discredits your theory. Why pull the shade, unscrew the bulb, and then leave the door open?"

Jim Sanders was suddenly grinning at Ellery. Sheila reached over and squeezed Jim's hand. He turned to smile at her. But his smile vanished as he heard Ellery say, "That clears Mr. Sanders of the second murder, but naturally it does not clear him of the first."

The sudden shrill ringing of the telephone caused everyone in the room, except Ellery, to start. Their nerves had been becoming more taut as each moment passed. They sat in tense silence while Ellery crossed the room and picked up the receiver. He listened, his face as inscrutable as those of the two Chinese sitting in the corner, looking as if they had only the mildest interest in the drama being enacted before them.

"Thanks," Ellery said quietly.

He returned to the door to the hall and once more faced the room. For a long interval of silence his gaze rested on Harry Walsh.

"Mr. Walsh, you have said that you did not know the exact day that Cobb was to arrive in

New York, and that you were informed of his arrival by Miss Cobb. Do you wish to alter that?"

"I do not, certainly not," Walsh said, and wiped his mouth with his handkerchief.

"You did not know what the mission was that Mr. Cobb had undertaken on behalf of the Chinese, is that so?"

"That is so. I've told the inspector that. Why do you ask?" He had begun to sweat profusely.

"This morning you denied knowing Corri. Do you still stick to that?"

Walsh frowned with impatience.

"I explained all that to you, Mr. Queen. I may have met him years ago—I can't be sure."

"Yet you called Corri 'Ritter,' without turning a hair."

Walsh was apparently unaware of the tide pouring down his neck. He had stopped mopping himself and sat staring belligerently at Ellery. He said nothing, apparently wondering whether he actually had called Corri "Ritter" or whether Ellery was trying to trick him. His doubt didn't last long.

"After leaving you this morning, Mr. Walsh,

I returned to your office. I found the door unlocked and took the liberty of looking at your old file.
You've known Corri or Ritter for years."

Walsh winced but recovered himself quickly.

"I told you my secretary may have handled
him. Besides, I've never heard of such impertinence."

Ellery's eyes suddenly seemed to take on the
quality of flint. They pierced into Walsh's.

"Mr. Walsh," he said slowly, "we are dealing
with murder. The penalty for murder is the electric chair. I shall give you a moment to weigh
your answers to my questions. You're going to
the penitentiary, anyhow. You've got only one
chance to escape the chair. If you're smart, you'll
take it."

The moments of silence while Ellery paused
were centennial. Once Walsh's lips moved, but
either he was unable to speak or changed his
mind, for no sound came from them.

Then Ellery began, "Mr. Walsh, Gordon Cobb
wrote you all about his being commissioned to
bring the Chinese treasure to this country. He

sent the letter to you by clipper. You destroyed the second part of the letter, but because of your cupidity you kept the first part, so that in case of his death—shall I say your murdering him?— you still could collect from his estate what he owed you. That was a costly mistake, as the first page clearly indicates that Mr. Cobb had told you his secret. Odd that you should be concerned about a few hundreds, when millions—and the chair—were at stake."

From his pocket, Ellery took the letter and held it up for Walsh to see.

"Now, do you come out with the whole story or shall I go on?"

Obviously, this time Walsh was unable to speak. He gaped at the letter until Ellery had restored it to his pocket.

"Furthermore," Ellery continued, "Gordon Cobb wired you from San Francisco. You signed the telegraph boy's book, acknowledging receipt of the wire." Again he reached into his pocket. This time he took out a copy of the telegram. He read it aloud: "Arriving August twelfth instead of fourteenth. Advise Sheila. Gordon Cobb."

Walsh's blotched face was distorted with terror as sweat streamed down it. His throat and mouth were as dry as the rest of him was wet. Again he made an effort to speak, but only a slight gurgle came from his lips.

Mercilessly Ellery continued, "The plan to rob Mr. Cobb of the jewels, Walsh, originated with you. You were the one person in this country, besides certain Support-for-China officers, who knew he was bringing them to America. But you couldn't handle the job alone. You had to have confederates. So you searched your mind for the most suitable crook. And that was Ritter. The nimble-fingered magician certainly had points in his favor. Then——"

Ellery stopped. Walsh was gesturing frantically to him. Finally he got partial control.

"I want—I want——" The words came as scarcely audible croaks.

"All right," Ellery snapped. Quickly he crossed to Brett. "And you, Brett," he said icily, "are you ready to talk, too?"

Brett was shaking as though he had suddenly become palsied. The color drained from his face. He nodded.

"Walsh murdered Cobb," he muttered huskily.

"No, he didn't, Brett," Ellery said quietly. "Are *you* ready to talk?"

CHAPTER XVIII

The Murderer

THERE was a sharp knock at the door. Ellery Queen went to it and partially opened it. Sergeant Velie was grinning at him.

"Wait till I call, Velie," he said and, closing the door, returned to Walsh. "How about it? Are you ready to come clean?"

Walsh nodded his head.

"And you, Brett?"

"I'll talk, Mr. Queen," Brett said, staring at the floor.

Ellery suddenly crossed to stand before R. M. Smith.

"Where were you, Mr. Smith, yesterday afternoon at the time Ritter was murdered?" he demanded.

Smith started.

"I didn't know that Ritter was dead until I heard you say so," he said uneasily. "He was murdered yesterday afternoon, you say. Well, I was at home all afternoon. My servant can prove that."

"Mr. Smith," said Ellery, "a few weeks ago Ritter came to you with Walsh's scheme to rob Gordon Cobb. The job couldn't be done without the proper organization. That's why Ritter went to you. He introduced you and Walsh. The loot was so huge there'd be plenty in it for all of you. You sent Brett to China with orders not to let Gordon Cobb out of his sight and to find out where he had concealed the jewels. Brett had a pretty good idea where they were hidden—it would be the logical place for Cobb to hide them.

"In searching Cobb's bedroom for it, the murderer was surprised by Cobb, and strangled him. The murderer hadn't found what he was looking for. He had to play for time, because he wasn't sure whether he'd been double-crossed by one of the gang or whether Cobb had been smart enough not to keep the jewels near him. All the murderer could be sure of was that what he was hunting for was not here in the apartment. He——"

"Wait a minute, Mr. Queen," Smith interrupted, "what you say about Brett, Walsh, Ritter, and me conspiring to rob Cobb is true. The trouble was that someone else was too smart for us. We weren't the only ones that got the bright idea. Well, we didn't succeed, so we didn't commit any crime. When we found out that Cobb had been murdered, we laid off. We don't go in for stuff like that. Well, you've got us cold, Mr. Queen. And like Walsh and Brett, I'm willing to come clean. We'll give you all the help we can."

"That's fine," said Ellery.

"You see, Mr. Queen," Smith continued, "I figure it like this. There are two possibilities. When we heard that Cobb had been murdered, we figured that some other bunch had got away with the jewels. Maybe they didn't, or maybe they did. Maybe Ritter put one over on us. Then they found out he had the jewels and croaked him."

"There was a woman named Olga Otero," Brett volunteered, "who was working for the other bunch."

Both he and Walsh had partially recovered their composure.

"Yes," Ellery agreed, "she's a member of a

foreign spy ring. The F. B. I. is taking care of her." He turned to Smith and said, "You're over-looking a third possibility."

"How do you figure that?" Smith looked per-plexed.

"That *you* murdered both Cobb and Ritter."

Smith gaped at Ellery.

"What do you mean?" he asked, frowning, "A joke's a joke, but——"

"Murder's never a joke, Smith." Ellery went to the door and opened it. "Out on the terrace," he whispered as Velie handed him a large cowhide bag. He set the bag down by the door.

Velie crossed the room and disappeared through the French window.

Smith leaped up from his chair, his eyes fixed on the bag.

"Smith," Ellery said, pointing at it, "this was in a trunk in your apartment. The trunk was locked. Sergeant Velie had to smash it open. I dare say the key is in your pocket now."

Smith's face was scarlet.

"I've never seen that before," he stammered. "Say, what is this?"

"You saw it yesterday afternoon when you

strangled Ritter," Ellery said evenly. "You sent him for the bag and told him to take it to his room. You were sure you'd find the jewels in it, concealed in what you couldn't find when you murdered Mr. Cobb. You unscrewed the bulb in Ritter's room and waited for him in the dark. You wanted the whole kit and boodle for yourself. You told Ritter that you and he would split it, double-crossing the others. But that wasn't your plan. A dead man can't talk. The tale you told me just now was what you planned to tell Brett and Walsh."

"It's a lie," Smith shouted. "It's a lie, and you can't pin a murder on me with just that bag as evidence."

"I don't plan to, Smith. You left your mark on Miss Cobb's wrist when you tried to snatch her bag. I suppose you thought her father might have mailed her a customs receipt for the jewels so that he wouldn't have it on him. You left your mark on Gordon Cobb when you strangled him. And you left it on Ritter's neck yesterday afternoon."

"What are you talking about?" He glared at Ellery.

Ellery exposed his right-hand palm to Smith.

With his left hand he squeezed the base of the index finger of the right. A red speck appeared. It grew larger until a globule of blood formed.

Suddenly Smith spun round. Like a madman he dashed through the French window and raced toward the parapet. In another second he would have dived into space had not Velie's enormous fist caught the point of his jaw. He staggered back, as if kicked. Then Ellery, with a flying tackle, struck him. Smith landed on the tiles with a crash that knocked him unconscious.

At Ellery Queen's request, the others remained after Smith, Walsh, and Brett had been taken to Police Headquarters. Smith was to be charged with two murders. What was to be charged against Walsh and Brett the inspector was glad to leave to the district attorney.

"But, son," he said, stroking his chin, "I still don't see how you knew it was Smith. Just how did you work it out?"

"It was pretty obvious, Dad," Ellery said, "when you consider the condition of Ritter's room. You remember that we noticed he couldn't have occupied it for several days as there was a thick coating of dust over everything, including the table below the light and the chair in the corner? The dust hadn't been disturbed anywhere except on the window sill, where we saw the streak."

"I don't get it, El," Velie interposed, scratching his head. "Now, if there had been fingerprints or footprints in the dust, I could——"

"That's exactly the point," Ellery interrupted. "The fact that there was none proved that someone reached up and turned the bulb without standing on the chair or the table. Now, as I told you, when I rescrewed it, I had to stand on tiptoe to reach it. No one under six feet could possibly reach it without standing on something, and either the table or the chair would be the logical thing to climb up on. Sanders is a head shorter than I am. That let him out. The only one of the suspects tall enough was Smith."

"But, Ellery," Nikki asked, "why did he suddenly want to commit suicide when he saw you squeeze a drop of blood out of your finger?"

"I was coming to that. Dad, remember those marked cards in Ritter's room?"

The inspector nodded.

"Remember your saying that not even a sleight of hand artist could palm a pin to mark them? He couldn't, but anyone could who'd had a needle-point set in the bottom of his ring. The first time I saw Smith he was playing cards and wearing a big signet ring. He was the only one who had a ring. After the game was over and Ritter was there alone, I saw him examine the backs of the cards. That's when he discovered how Smith did it. He took the pack, probably to have proof ready the next time Smith swindled him and the other members of the gang.

"Naturally, Smith would have to wear the ring constantly. He wouldn't dare leave it lying around where someone might pick it up and see the needle-point. Of course, he couldn't have realized that he'd scratched Miss Cobb and his victims until I told him about this mark."

"Oh," Sheila gasped. "That's what scratched me!"

"But, Ellery," Nikki said, wide-eyed, "I don't see how you could squeeze the blood out of your finger."

Inspector Queen laughed.

"Well, I do," he said, "and El was pretty smart

about it. It was when you shook hands with him just after he got here, wasn't it?"

"Yes, I gripped his hand hard with my index finger pressed against the bottom of the ring. I felt the prick all right. Then I knew that all we needed was the evidence of his possession of the bag to prove him the murderer." He turned to the sergeant. "That was good work, Velie. The fact that it was locked up in Smith's trunk clinches the case."

"I was pretty dumb not to know what was in the bag," Velie admitted shamefacedly. "I felt like a fool when I saw it."

"Oh, Mr. Queen," Lois Ling said excitedly. "Do you mean the jewels are in it?" She stared at the bag, which was still where Ellery had set it near the door to the hall.

Ellery shook his head.

"I'd be the most surprised person in the world if they were," he said sadly.

"The ice ain't there," Velie announced.

Inspector Queen frowned.

"Ellery, what *is* in the bag?"

Ellery shook his head.

"To think that my own father—a police inspector——" He groaned. "Oh, Dad, what of Cobb's has been so obviously missing that it fairly shouted at you?"

The inspector snorted and blew through his mustache.

"What?" he demanded.

"Dad, what does a ventriloquist always have?"

"Oof!" Inspector Queen clapped his hand to his face. "Sergeant, we're two fools!"

"Oh," Nikki piped up, "of course! The dummy. Mr. Cobb's dummy."

Ellery nodded.

"He undoubtedly hid the jewels in it when he brought them from China."

"And they're gone? Really gone?" Lois Ling asked, looking at the sergeant as if she couldn't bring herself to believe it.

"Sorry, Miss," he said sympathetically.

Lois Ling could not conceal her agitation.

"But they meant so much, so awfully much to millions of——" She dropped her arms resignedly and turned to her father, speaking to him in Chinese.

"Dad," Ellery said, "the ancient method of reckoning time in China was to divide the day into twelve intervals of two hours each. The interval of the pig was between 9 and 11 P. M.; the interval of the serpent, between 9 and 11 A. M.; and so on. The names of animals were used for all twelve. When I saw the cards that had been sent to Cobb, I realized they must have been printed by a Chinese. The thick strokes were made with a brush. Who but a Chinese would use a brush to write with? So I called up a Chinese scholar and I found that the interval from 3 to 5 P. M. was designated by the word Monkey."

Inspector Queen blinked.

"That's why you wanted me to have that ad put in the Chinese paper."

"For the black hand man?" Nikki asked excitedly.

"Of course not," Ellery said. "It's pretty obvious that someone was trying to communicate with Mr. Cobb in a code they had prearranged between them. The man must be some Chinese friend who didn't know that Cobb was no longer alive. The ad was to invite him to come here between three and five. It's three-thirty now. He may arrive any minute."

Lois Ling turned quickly to Ellery.

"Mr. Queen, there's hope?"

"Perhaps. After we got a break in getting back Miss Cobb's jade necklace, why not——"

"Ellery," Sheila interrupted, "did Miss Otero steal the necklace?" She put her hand to her throat and fingered the pendant.

"You can be certain he never gave it to her," Sanders said positively.

Ellery started to say something, but stopped when they heard a knock at the door.

"Come in," he called.

The door opened, and an aged Chinese stepped into the room. He turned his wrinkled face slowly and looked wonderingly at the people in the room.

"Missa Cobb? Missa Cobb?" he asked, and then, seeing the bag, started.

CHAPTER XIX

THE DUMMY

LOIS LING and her father crossed quickly to the newcomer. For several minutes they talked rapidly in Chinese. Then Lois turned to Inspector Queen.

"This is Li Soo," she explained. "He doesn't speak English. He saw the ad. He didn't know that Mr. Cobb was dead. He'd been trying to get in touch with him."

"Ask him if the jewels were in the bag," Ellery said.

She turned back to Li Soo.

After a moment or two, Lois Ling said, "Mr. Cobb hid the jewels in the dummy. Li Soo came over on the boat with him. He was disguised as a laundryman. At sea, Mr. Cobb gave him the bag to bring through the customs. Mr. Cobb knew there were foreign agents aboard, watching him. Li Soo remained aboard two days after the ship reached San Francisco. Mr. Cobb acted as a decoy to lure the agents East while he——"

Li Soo said something to her in Chinese. Although Ellery could understand nothing, he saw that Li Soo was greatly agitated.

"He says he must open the bag at once," Lois Ling said to the inspector.

Inspector Queen nodded. Li Soo got down on his knees beside the bag. The lock had been forced. He unfastened the two brass catches, jerked the bag open and, getting up, lifted out the ventriloquist's dummy.

The beautifully carved wooden head of the Chinese dummy was hollow, with movable eyes and lips. The long black hair, surmounted by a ceremonial headdress, was human hair. The dummy was dressed in a voluminous gown of pale blue silk, embroidered in yellow, violet, and green.

Carefully Li Soo laid it on the table. Reaching up under the gown, he worked his hand down one of the hollow arms. Suddenly his eyes brightened. He drew out a sheet of paper, examined it quickly, and handed it to Lois Ling, speaking rapidly in Chinese.

Lois Ling's face lit up as she turned to Inspector Queen.

"Li Soo," she explained, "forwarded the jewels

in bond to New York. The duty was to be paid here. This is the customs receipt. To fool anyone who might inquire if Gordon Cobb had declared the jewels or forwarded them in bond, he had the receipt made out in the name of Sheila Ventro. He left the bag downstairs for Mr. Cobb, knowing that the jewels could be taken out of bond only by Miss Cobb. Mr. Cobb was to have her endorse the receipt over to the Support-for-China Society. When Li Soo didn't hear from Mr. Cobb, he tried to get in touch with him and sent the coded messages."

It seemed to Ellery that Sheila was as pleased as Lois Ling, her father, and Li Soo about the safety of the jewels. She arranged to meet Lois Ling and the officials of the Chinese organization the following morning at the Customs House. She was obviously proud that she could consummate the mission her father had begun. But the emotional strain of the past two days had told on her. She turned impulsively to Jim Sanders for sympathy and support. After Lois Ling left with her father and Li Soo, Jim Sanders took Sheila out onto the terrace. Only time, he realized, could lessen her grief, her sense of loss. Now she must be distracted as much as possible. She must think of other things—of the future.

With large eyes, Nikki watched Jim and Sheila as they leaned against the parapet, looking out over the city. She sighed and turned her gaze to Ellery, who was deep in conversation with his father and Velie. He was so dynamic, she decided. Or was that the word? So vital, so full of energy—so exasperatingly male. She continued to watch him, half smiling, proud of him. Finally the discussion was over and all the finer points explained. The inspector and Velie went away.

Sheila and Jim came in from the terrace, and Sheila went to the bedroom to powder her nose. Jim incoherently tried to thank Ellery, who promptly stopped him.

Then Jim grinned self-consciously and said, glancing toward the bedroom, "Well, I think maybe I've a chance—a chance to be the luckiest man in the world, if I've got it in me. Gosh, she's a wonderful person." He changed the subject abruptly. "The view's perfectly grand from up here. You can see clear across to the Palisades."

Nikki gave him a quick fleeting smile of sympathy and went to join Sheila.

To Ellery's surprise, a moment or two later, Sheila appeared without Nikki. After a few words with Ellery, she asked Jim if he'd see her home, and hurried him off.

Shortly after the door closed behind them, he heard Nikki call.

"Oh, Ellery! Come here. I'm on the terrace."

Now what? he wondered as he started for the terrace.

Nikki took her elbows off the parapet as he came up to her. She linked an arm through his.

"Look down at the park," she said. "Isn't it lovely? They're sailing little boats on the lake."

"So they are," said Ellery.

"How green the trees are. It's like a beautiful green tapestry."

Ellery sniffed. Then he grinned. While she was in the bedroom she must have put some *muguet* scent on her golden-brown hair. Distinctly it gave out waves of lily of the valley.

Nikki lowered her voice and turned her big brown eyes up at him.

"It is so—beautifully romantic."

"It is—romantic," he agreed.

She pressed his arm closer.

"Nikki," he said slowly, "I suppose this is the wrong time to bring it up—but will you come away with me?"

"Ellery," she breathed.

"I mean now."

"Oh, Ellery! If you really want me to——"

"I do. Really. It's just about four."

She glanced at her wrist watch.

"Five to." Her face was like a child's; eager.

"Well, let's go."

"But where, Ellery? It's so late this afternoon."

"To the office," said Mr. Queen grimly. "It's not too late. You can still get in a good hour's work on my manuscript!"

CPSIA information can be obtained
at www.ICGtesting.com
Printed in the USA
LVHW040819100219
607010LV00034B/855/P

9 781258 209742